Pike Place
Public Market
Seafood
Cookbook

PIKE PLACE
PUBLIC MARKET
SEAFOOD
COOKBOOK

Second Edition

Braiden Rex-Johnson

Photography by **Jeff Koehler**

TEN SPEED PRESS
Berkeley | Toronto

To our beloved Beauregard (Bo-Bo) Johnson,
a feline who never met a singing scallop or
Dungeness crab he didn't like.
November 22, 1988–August 10, 2004

Ten Speed Press
P.O. Box 7123
Berkeley, California, 94707

Distributed in Australia by Simon and Schuster Australia,
in Canada by Ten Speed Press Canada, in New Zealand by Southern Publishers Group,
in South Africa by Real Books, and in the United Kingdom
and Europe by Airlift Book Company.

Cover and Interior Design by Cathey Flickinger

Library of Congress Cataloging-in-Publication Data is on file with the publisher

ISBN-10: 1-58008-680-2
ISBN-13: 978-1-58008-680-6

First printing, 2005

Printed in China
1 2 3 4 5 6 7 8 9 10 — 09 08 07 06 05

CONTENTS

INTRODUCTION

Cookbooks are a lot like children. They take at least nine months to produce, come out with great fanfare, then sink or swim depending on their merit. So it was quite a thrill when the first edition of the *Pike Place Public Market Seafood Cookbook* came out in 1997, earned good reviews, and went on to sell 20,000 copies around the world.

In 2004, when the editors at Ten Speed Press asked me to choose the 50 best recipes for an abridged edition of the original, I was (naturally) elated. What mother wouldn't crave the chance to revisit and refashion a beloved child into a snappy, streamlined version?

But as I started working, my conscience flared. I realized my new book would never, could never be anything like the original. Even back in 1997, certain fish species were being overfished or caught as bycatch (a term that means unintended catch, such as juvenile fish, marine birds, or sea turtles) almost to the point of extinction. I purposefully excluded them from my book's encyclopedic listing of fish.

Today, many other fish species highlighted in my original book are now squarely on the "endangered" list. In fact, the Marine Stewardship Council (MSC; msc.org), an international nonprofit organization that promotes sustainable fisheries, estimates that overfishing occurs in 60 percent of the world's stocks.

But the news is not all grim. Here in the Pacific Northwest, our wild salmon stocks are well managed and safe to eat. In fact, the MSC recognized Alaskan salmon as the first United States fishery to be certified as sustainable. Only fisheries that meet strict, peer-reviewed standards of sustainability can qualify. Alaskan salmon is now eligible to bear the MSC eco-label, which lets consumers know that when they buy MSC-labeled seafood, they are supporting healthier oceans and a healthier environment. Alaskan halibut is also in wide supply, as are the state's prime weathervane scallops and spot prawns.

Environmentally friendly farm-raised clams, mussels, and oysters line our shores. Their innovative cultivation techniques have resulted in the Monterey Bay Aquarium and other environmental groups rating Northwest-grown clams, mussels, and oysters at the top of their "green" list. Even geoducks, the largest clams in North America, have recently been successfully (and profitably) farmed for the first and only time in the world in Northwest waters.

Albacore tuna remains a widely available summertime treat for the grill. Farm-raised Idaho trout is also in excellent supply. And crabs from the carefully managed Dungeness crab fishery are not only a joy, but safe, to eat.

The finfish and shellfish varieties highlighted in the recipes in this book are (so far) safe to buy and eat. And the task of choosing safe, sustainable seafood has grown much easier thanks to groups such as the Monterey Bay Aquarium and the National Audubon Society, which produce guides listing the types of currently sustainable seafood. Fish swim on and off the charts and the charts don't always agree, so check out the Web sites at audubon.org or mbayaq.org for the latest listings.

In addition to careful selection of seafood, here are half a dozen other easy ways to conserve our ocean's resources, while saving your pocketbook as well.

FROM THE HEART of WASHINGTON

Green Beans
$ 1⁰⁰ /lb.

- **Buy fish in season.** When large quantities of a fish or shellfish are running and widely available, they are often sold at bargain prices. For example, fresh wild salmon caught during the bountiful summer and early fall runs is much less expensive than salmon caught during the winter months.

- **Buy fish that are less well known or popular.** Everybody knows how delicious fresh king salmon can be, but how many people have tried lesser-known species, such as coho or keta? Or how about farm-raised trout, tilapia, or catfish?

- **Serve smaller portions of finfish.** Because seafood is a lean, pure protein with very little waste (especially if you buy fish fillets rather than steaks), consider serving it in smaller portions than you might chicken or beef. Not too long ago eight ounces of finfish (such as salmon or halibut) was considered an average-size portion. Nowadays, many Americans actually get too much protein in their diets; I find that for myself and my husband, anywhere from four to six ounces of finfish is just enough, while for a family of four, often one to one-and-one-half pounds is adequate.

- **When dining out,** order a seafood appetizer (or two) as your entrée. Or order a seafood entrée, eat only half, and ask for a "to-go" box for the rest. I have been using the latter technique for years, mostly because I can never finish the typically gargantuan portions (sometimes upwards of eight to ten ounces) offered at many restaurants. I eat my leftovers the next day for lunch, or freeze them for later use in seafood stews or soups. And ordering several seafood appetizers in place of a main course is one of the least wasteful and inexpensive (not to mention fun!) ways to experiment with and experience a variety of seafood dishes.

- **Serve seafood as a supporting part of a meal.** When combined with an "extender," such as potatoes, pasta, grains, or vegetables, much less seafood per person is needed. Seafood chili, pasta, and risotto are just a few suggestions of how to serve smaller portions of seafood while still providing satisfying meals. This is also a healthful way to eat, since grains (particularly whole grains) and beans provide much-needed doses of soluble and insoluble fiber. See the Seafood Combination Dishes section (page 108) for full-blown examples.

- **Use seafood combinations** to "stretch" your dollar. When making seafood dishes, use a variety of finfish and shellfish. For example, mix Alaskan spot prawns (an expensive choice) with farm-raised mussels and/or clams and fresh halibut (typically less expensive choices) to cut costs.

With a little thoughtful planning on our part today, generations to come will continue to savor the healthful and satisfying bounty of our vibrant Northwest waters. And our consciences will be the better for it.

Braiden Rex-Johnson
March 2005

PART I

A FISH LOVER'S PRIMER

A BRIEF HISTORY OF PIKE PLACE FISH MARKETS

Seafood has always been a hot commodity along Seattle's Pike Place. During the 1920s and 1930s, there were eleven fish stalls inside the Market. Today, the number of fish stalls is fewer, but the stalls are larger and better stocked. The four fresh fish stores and one smoked fish store in the Market each has its own specialties, "personality," and unique history. Locals in search of dinner and tourists seeking the freshest Northwest salmon or other goodies to take with them or to ship to the folks back home shop with the appropriate fishmonger based on their needs and desires.

Pure Food Fish was one of the original fish stores in the Market, opened in 1917. Present owner Sol Amon has been in charge since 1959, when he took over from his father, Jack, who began working at Pike Place fish markets in 1911. Look for the blackboard behind the counter for the ever-changing list of fresh fish and shellfish, then ask for recipe suggestions when buying from the helpful fishmongers at Pure Food Fish.

Pike Place Fish is nicknamed "the home of low-flying fish" because its vociferous fishmongers entertain the crowds with sea chanties and acrobatic throws of everything from huge whole salmon to bags of singing scallops. Established in 1930, Pike Place Fish has been owned since 1965 by Johnny Yokoyama, who started in the Market at the age of eight working at his parents' fresh produce stall.

Jack's Fish Spot stands out as the only fish stall in the Market boasting both fresh shellfish tanks and a small seafood bar. Owner Jack Mathers has been in the Market since 1982, although the space was once home to Philadelphia Fish Market, one of the original Pike Place Public Market fish stores, which closed in 1969.

Totem Smokehouse is the only store in the Market devoted exclusively to smoked seafood such as hot-smoked salmon, oysters, rainbow trout, and albacore tuna, and cold-smoked Nova lox.

City Fish lays claim to the most intriguing fish tale in the Market. It was started by the city council of Seattle in 1918 when the price of salmon had skyrocketed to a whopping twenty-five cents per pound. Although city intervention helped bring the price of a pound of salmon down to just ten cents, the city decided to bail out after several years of marginal profits.

David Levy, nicknamed "Good Weight Dave" by his appreciative customers, bought the business in 1922 and turned it into a Market institution symbolized by the bright neon fish atop its roof. Good Weight Dave's descendants continued to run City Fish until February 1995, when former Alaska fisherman Jon Daniels, a strapping young man with eyes as blue-gray as the ocean and a viselike handshake forged by years at sea, took over the business.

Any of the fish stalls in the Market will pack seafood in leak-proof, odor-proof containers lined with "blue ice" frozen gel packs. The containers are guaranteed to keep the contents fresh up to 48 hours. They are designed to carry on the plane or check as luggage, or can be shipped by overnight air express. Because of the extraordinary care that must be taken when shipping fresh seafood, the quality of air-shipped fish rivals that of fish just out of the case at the local seafood market.

Whichever fishmonger you choose, the essence of the Pike Place Public Market fish stalls stays the same—to sell fresh Northwest seafood with a bit of the old, hard sell, a sense of artistry and showmanship, and a plethora of expertise and dedication—all of which are treasured by tourists and locals alike.

FUN FACT

Fresh fish at the Market is displayed on ice in open trays. When the City of Seattle threatened to force the fishmongers to put their wares behind glass to meet health code requirements, a special ordinance was passed by the Health Department in 1979 to keep the fish on ice and out in front.

SEAFOOD BASICS 101:
CHOOSING AND STORING FISH

SEAFOOD is one of the most perishable of all fresh foods and must be handled with great care. Following are general guidelines for seafood selection and storage.

Selecting a Seafood Market

PERHAPS THE MOST IMPORTANT decision when buying fresh seafood is the place you purchase it. Consider the following factors when deciding where to buy your seafood.

- First, smell the place—it should not have a fishy odor.

- Look at the number of customers; the faster the turnover of product, the fresher the fish.

- The labeling on the fish should be clear and specific. "Sockeye salmon steaks" is much more helpful than merely "salmon."

- Finfish should be displayed separately from shellfish, and raw separately from cooked, to avoid contamination.

- The ice in which the fish is displayed should be clean and white. Whole fish should be in plenty of fresh, clean ice. Cut fish should not sit directly on ice, but rather in trays placed over ice.

- The market should cut its own fish.

- The staff should be able to answer questions knowledgeably and offer good culinary recommendations.

General Shopping Tips

- WHEN SHOPPING, purchase seafood last and take it home immediately. Don't stop to run a few additional errands on the way home or the seafood will suffer in quality.

- Never let seafood sit unrefrigerated for long, especially in a hot car. If it is over 30 minutes from your seafood shop to your home, ask that your seafood be packed with a separate bag of ice or frozen gel packs (also known as "blue ice" packs), or bring along a cooler filled with ice or frozen gel packs.

- Make friends with your fishmonger. A friendly face behind the seafood counter may be your best insurance of sparkling fish on the plate. Let your fish-

monger know you want and can discern the highest quality fish; good fish-mongers respect and appreciate knowledgeable clients.

- Call ahead with special orders and requirements; when a fish market delivers the goods, call back and express your thanks.

- Ask questions and share your knowledge and recipes with your fishmonger.

- If the seafood you purchase doesn't meet your expectations, take it back immediately and explain why it is less than perfect. A good fishmonger will be glad to replace the questionable product with something to your liking.

Purchasing Whole Fish

- THE OLD RULES suggested that clear, bright eyes in a whole fish meant a fresh fish. Unfortunately, the eyes of some species go cloudy very quickly, while others stay clear long past the time that the fish is fresh. Eye condition is not infallible and should be considered as just one of several indicators of freshness.

- Flesh should be firm, springy, and shiny; dull flesh may mean the fish is old. The flesh should be plump, not separating from the bones. A very fresh fish will have a bright, reflective slime on its surface.

- The gills, if still in the fish, should be vivid red or pink and free of mucus. Brownish or grayish gills are a sign of age. However, if the fish has been bled, the gills will have lost their bright color.

- The intestinal cavity should be clean and pink. If you are allowed to pick up the fish before buying it, sniff the stomach cavity and gills for "off" odors. High-quality fish should smell clean, fresh, and almost sweet.

- The fish should have most of its scales. Avoid fish with bruises, puncture marks, or ragged fins, for these telltale signs of mishandling mean the fish will deteriorate more rapidly.

- Headless fish should not have brown edges.

Purchasing Cut Fish

- WHEN PURCHASING FISH fillets or steaks, look for a clear, bright, translucent glow and a luminous, shimmering color in the flesh, which should not be milky.

- The flesh should be moist, firm, and elastic to the touch, with no darkening around the edges of the fish, brown or yellowish discoloration, a dull or opaque color, blood spots, or dry or mushy areas.

- Smell the fillets or steaks—they should have no fishy, ammonia, or chemical odor.

- The knife work should be sharp and even—steaks cut with sloping sides (known as shingle cuts) or fillets with jagged edges cook unevenly and should be avoided. Steaks should be cut to an even thickness, depending on the type of species and the way it cooks.

- If the fish has been prepackaged (placed in a Styrofoam tray and overwrapped in plastic), it should be tightly wrapped with little or no air and no liquid in the packaging.

Portion Size

BECAUSE SEAFOOD IS A GIFT from the sea to be treasured with every bite, in general the recipes in this book allow about 5 to 6 ounces of usable flesh per serving for main courses and 4 ounces when the seafood is combined with other ingredients.

As a general rule, purchase 3/4 to 1 pound of whole fish per entrée-size serving; 1/2 pound of pan-dressed (cleaned) fish or fish steaks per portion; and 1/3 pound of skin-on or skinless fish fillets per serving. About 1/2 pound of shellfish meats makes 1 serving; 1 1/4 to 1 1/2 pounds of live lobster, crab, or crawfish per entrée portion; 1 1/2 to 2 pounds of live mussels or clams per serving; 2 1/2 to 3 pounds of live oysters per serving; 1 pound of whole, head-on shrimp per serving; or 1/2 to 3/4 pound of shrimp with the shells on and heads removed per serving.

Storage

· REFRIGERATE SEAFOOD as soon as possible at 32°F. Although this temperature is cooler than most home refrigerators, it can be achieved by placing whole fish, fish fillets, or steaks in resealable plastic bags. Press out as much air as possible from each bag, seal the bag, and roll up the fish in the remaining portion of the bag. Place a layer of ice in a container large enough to hold the plastic bag without crowding. Place the bag over ice, then cover with more ice. Set the container in the coldest section of the refrigerator (usually the bottom back shelf), drain the ice as it melts, and refresh with new ice as needed. A nice alternative is to store the plastic bags between layers of "blue ice" packs. Fresh fish stored in this way will keep for one to two days, twice as long as fish stored at 37°F. However, if you cannot use the fish within a day or two, freeze it immediately, provided it has not been previously frozen.

· Before cooking fresh seafood, rinse under cold water and pat dry with paper towels.

· Do not leave raw or cooked seafood unrefrigerated for more than 2 hours, including preparation time and time on the table.

Part II

Finfish

Halibut with Sundried Tomato Tapenade

TAPENADE is a thick paste traditionally made of capers, anchovies, ripe olives, olive oil, lemon juice, and seasonings. My bright, lemony version offers a bold contrast in color, taste, and texture to mild-flavored, simply broiled halibut.

1 cup oil-packed sundried tomatoes, drained and coarsely chopped

1/2 cup pimiento-stuffed green olives, coarsely chopped

1 teaspoon capers

1 clove garlic, cut in half

Zest of 1 lemon

Juice of 1 lemon

Tabasco sauce

1 1/2 pounds halibut fillets, 1/2 to 3/4 inches thick, bones removed, rinsed, drained, patted dry, and cut into 4 (6-ounce) pieces

Salt and freshly ground black pepper

1 tablespoon olive oil

Preheat broiler. Lightly coat a baking sheet with oil or nonstick cooking spray.

Place the sundried tomatoes, olives, capers, garlic, and lemon zest in a mini-food processor and process until minced, or mince the ingredients by hand. Place the minced vegetables and lemon juice in a small nonreactive mixing bowl and stir well. Season to taste with Tabasco, cover, and set aside at room temperature.

Sprinkle halibut fillets lightly with salt and pepper. Place fillets onprepared baking sheet and brush lightly with olive oil. Place fish 3 to 4 inches under broiler. Broil 5 to 7 minutes, depending on thickness of fillets, or just until they turn opaque.

When the fillets are done, divide among individual plates. Spoon 2 tablespoons of the sundried tomato mixture beside each fillet.

Serves 4

HALIBUT WINES

With its lean, flavorful, slightly sweet meat and distinctive taste, not to mention its firm, dense texture and large flakes, halibut is an authoritative white fish that pairs well with many different wines.

Simply grilled, its buttery texture and slight char from the fire makes it a good candidate with an oaky Chardonnay. Take that same grilled fish, top it with a citrus beurre blanc, and it would pair better with a lean, unoaked Chardonnay with lemon-citrus undertones. Sauvignon Blanc or Sémillon would also suit.

Halibut chunks are often added to the Northwest cioppino pot, where the tomato-based broth makes for pleasant sipping with fruity red wines, such as Merlot, Syrah, or Zinfandel.

Poached Halibut with Spicy Mashed Potatoes

MASHED POTATOES have become all the rage in upscale restaurants across the country. I add Asian elements to my rendition and like to top a heaping mound of the spicy potatoes with a tender poached halibut fillet.

> 1 pound baking potatoes, peeled and cut into 1 1/2-inch chunks
>
> 2 cloves garlic, peeled and cut in half, plus 2 cloves garlic, peeled and crushed
>
> 1 teaspoon toasted sesame oil
>
> 1/4 teaspoon Thai red curry paste
>
> 1/2 cup fat-free, 1/3-less-sodium chicken stock (see note)
>
> 2 teaspoons soy sauce
>
> 1 cup water
>
> 1 cup dry white wine
>
> 1 1/2 pounds halibut fillets, skin and bones removed, rinsed, drained, patted dry, and cut into 4 (6-ounce) pieces
>
> Steamed brussels sprouts, broccoli florets, or 1/4-inch-thick carrot rounds (optional)

To make mashed potatoes, place the potatoes and the 2 cloves peeled and halved garlic in a saucepan and cover with several inches of cold water. Bring to a boil and cook 15 to 20 minutes, or until the potatoes are tender. Drain well, then put the potatoes and garlic through a ricer, or mash with a fork.

In a small bowl, mix the toasted sesame oil, red curry paste, chicken stock, and soy sauce until smooth. Add to potatoes, mix well, cover, and keep warm.

To poach the fish, bring the water, wine, and crushed garlic to a boil in a skillet large enough to hold the fillets without crowding them. Remove the pan from the heat, add the halibut fillets, return to heat, reduce heat to low, partially cover (set the lid slightly askew so that steam can escape), and simmer 5 to 10 minutes, or until the fish just turns opaque. Do not allow the water to boil. Remove the fish fillets and place on several layers of paper towels to drain well.

To serve, scoop a mound of mashed potatoes in the center of individual plates and place a halibut fillet over the potatoes. If desired, arrange steamed vegetables in a circle around the mashed potatoes.

Serves 4

Note: *If fat-free, $^1/_3$-less-sodium chicken stock is unavailable, substitute defatted chicken stock and omit the 2 teaspoons soy sauce.*

Hot Honeyed Halibut

Mech Apiaries, Pike Place Public Market

DORIS AND DON MECH founded Mech Apiaries in 1973, and every Saturday, Doris brings a wide range of Washington-state-grown honey and honey products to the Market's North Arcade. This recipe was inspired by Doris's delightful book, *Joy with Honey.*

> 2 tablespoons honey
> $^1/_2$ teaspoon Tabasco sauce
> 2 tablespoons low-sodium soy sauce
> 1 tablespoon freshly squeezed lemon juice
> 1 tablespoon vegetable oil or canola oil
> 1$^1/_2$ pounds halibut fillets, bones removed, rinsed, drained, patted dry,
>   and cut into 4 (6-ounce) pieces

In a small bowl, stir together the honey, Tabasco, soy sauce, and lemon juice. Reserve mixture for later use.

Heat the oil in a large skillet over medium-high heat. Add the halibut fillets flesh side down (skin side up) and cook for 3 to 5 minutes. Turn over the fillets and cook for 3 to 5 minutes more, or about 10 minutes per inch of thickness. During the last 2 minutes of cooking, drizzle the reserved honey mixture evenly over the fillets.

When the fillets just turn opaque, divide them among individual plates and serve immediately.

Serves 4

Halibut Nuggets with Hazelnut Crumb Crust

LUSCIOUS HAZELNUTS, from Washington and Oregon orchards, elevate chunks of halibut to new heights in this easy recipe.

> 2 tablespoons Dijon mustard
> 2 tablespoons soy sauce
> 2 tablespoons butter, melted
> 1 tablespoon honey
> 1/4 cup Panko bread crumbs or unseasoned dry bread crumbs (see page 127)
> 1/4 cup finely chopped hazelnuts
> 2 teaspoons minced cilantro, plus extra sprigs for garnish
> 1 1/2 pounds halibut fillets, skin and bones removed, rinsed, drained, patted dry,
>   and cut into 16 pieces
> Salt and freshly ground black pepper
> 3 cups cooked jasmine or basmati rice

Preheat oven to 450°F. Lightly coat a baking sheet with oil or nonstick cooking spray. Set the baking sheet aside.

In a small mixing bowl, stir together the mustard, soy sauce, butter, and honey. In another small bowl, mix together the bread crumbs, hazelnuts, and the minced cilantro.

Lightly sprinkle the halibut pieces with salt and pepper. Dip the top of each halibut nugget in the honey-mustard mixture, allow the excess to drain off, then dip in the hazelnut-crumb mixture. Place the nuggets on the baking sheet without crowding.

Bake the halibut nuggets for 8 to 12 minutes, or 10 minutes per inch of thickness. The fish should just turn opaque. To test for doneness, cut into the center of one nugget with the tip of a small, sharp knife and pull apart slightly.

To serve, mound the rice in the center of individual plates. Place the nuggets in a symmetrical pattern over the rice mounds and garnish with the cilantro sprigs.

Serves 4

Note: *Panko bread crumbs are lightly colored, coarsely textured crumbs used in Japanese cooking to coat fried foods. They are available in Asian markets and the Asian section of most grocery stores.*

FUN FACT

Halibut is one of the oldest commercial fisheries on the West Coast, dating back to 1888. Fishers with names such as Rotten Robert, Long and Narrow, and Blood Poison Bill searched for halibut in schooners. They were paid by the number of halibut they caught, exchanging the fish tongues for pay at the end of the day.

Balsamic-Glazed Salmon

Il Bistro, Pike Place Public Market

THE MUSKY, yet sweet taste of balsamic vinegar pairs perfectly with the fatty flesh of salmon. The balsamic glaze is good on other types of seafood as well, particularly on sablefish or Alaskan weathervane scallops.

> *2 tablespoons olive oil*
> *1 1/2 pounds salmon fillets, bones removed, rinsed, drained, patted dry,*
> *   and cut into 4 (6-ounce) pieces*
> *1 clove garlic, chopped*
> *2 plum tomatoes, cored and sliced 1/4 inch thick*
> *2 tablespoons freshly squeezed lemon juice*
> *1/4 cup balsamic vinegar*
> *1/2 cup fish stock or chicken stock*
> *2 tablespoons butter*
> *3 tablespoons basil chiffonade (see page 125)*

Preheat oven to 425°F. Lightly coat a baking dish large enough to hold the salmon fillets without crowding with oil or nonstick cooking spray.

Heat olive oil over medium-high heat in a skillet large enough to hold the salmon fillets without crowding. (Alternatively, use two skillets or cook salmon in two batches.) When oil is hot but not smoking, add salmon fillets, flesh side down, and cook 3 minutes, or until fish is golden brown outside but still rare inside. Place the salmon in the reserved baking dish skin side down and place in the oven for 8 to 10 minutes or until the fish just turns opaque.

(continued)

Return the skillet to medium-high heat and add the garlic, tomatoes, lemon juice, balsamic vinegar, and fish stock. Cook until reduced to 3 to 4 tablespoons, stirring occasionally. Remove from the heat and add the butter and basil, swirling to blend.

To serve, divide the salmon fillets among warmed individual plates and drizzle with glaze.

Serves 4

Richard's Copper River Salmon Croquettes

Pure Food Fish, Pike Place Public Market

IN MAY AND JUNE, when Copper River kings are running, Richard Hoage, a close friend and trusted fishmonger, occasionally saves some meaty bones as a special treat. I take them home and scrape away the succulent nubbins of flesh, then use Richard's recipe to make salmon croquettes.

> *1 egg*
> *Pinch of salt*
> *Pinch of freshly ground black or white pepper*
> *2 cloves garlic, minced*
> *1/2 onion, diced*
> *2 tablespoons minced flat-leaf parsley, or 1 tablespoon minced cilantro, plus additional*
> *   sprigs for garnish*
> *1 pound Copper River salmon meat, or 1 pound salmon fillet, skin and bones removed,*
> *   minced by hand or food processor*
> *1 to 1 1/2 cups unseasoned soft bread crumbs (see page 127)*
> *1 tablespoon olive oil, or 1 1/2 teaspoons olive oil and 1 1/2 teaspoons unsalted butter*
> *Lemon wedges, for garnish*

In a large mixing bowl, stir together the egg, salt, pepper, garlic, onion, and the minced parsley. Add the salmon and stir gently until the egg mixture is well incorporated. Add 1 cup of the bread crumbs and stir again. If the salmon mixture is still too sticky to handle, add the remaining bread crumbs and stir again. Divide the salmon into 4 portions and form into patties. Do not handle the salmon any more than absolutely necessary.

Over medium heat, place a nonstick skillet large enough to hold the patties without crowding. When the pan is hot, add the olive oil. When the oil is hot but not smoking, add the patties and cook 5 minutes, or until lightly browned. Turn and cook 3 to 5 minutes more, or until the patties just turn opaque in the middle. Alternately, the patties can be baked on a lightly greased baking sheet in a 400°F oven for 6 to 8 minutes on each side, or until the patties are lightly browned, or broil 4 to 6 inches from the heat source for 4 to 5 minutes on each side.

Transfer the croquettes to individual plates, garnish with the parsley sprigs and lemon wedges, and serve.

Serves 4

FUN FACT

According to Northwest Native Americans, salmon were spirit people living in a magic village under the sea who were sent upriver to feed the human race. Indeed, in several native languages, the word for fish is the same as the word for salmon. Each year, the people prayed for the salmon to return. The arrival of the salmon was anticipated with eagerness, because it meant that the dried fish of winter could be replaced with succulent fresh salmon. Only after the bones of the first salmon were returned to the river, ensuring their annual return, could the harvest begin. Today, as in ancient times, the arrival of the first spring Chinook creates excitement among Native Americans in the Northwest.

Steamed Salmon Cantonese Style

Wild Ginger, Seattle, Washington

WHEN SALMON IS STEAMED with fresh ginger, fish sauce, and premium rice wine, it takes on a creamy texture that cannot be achieved with any other cooking method. As a final step, hot, garlic-flavored oil is poured over the salmon to sear in the juices.

3 cups water
1/2 pound salmon fillets, bones removed, rinsed, drained, patted dry, and cut into
    2 (4-ounce) pieces
1/2-inch length gingerroot, very thinly sliced
2 tablespoons Shao Hsing Chinese rice wine or mirin
2 tablespoons Thai fish sauce (nam pla)
2 to 3 tablespoons peanut oil
1 clove garlic
2 green onions, top 2 inches removed, remaining portion julienned
2 sprigs cilantro, for garnish

To steam in a wok, cross two chopsticks in an X, then cut a groove in the lower chopstick so that the top one fits snugly. Set the chopsticks in the wok and add water to 1 inch below the level of the chopsticks. Place lid on wok and turn heat to high.

Place the salmon, skin side down, on a glass pie plate or rimmed glass plate slightly smaller than the diameter of the wok. Cover with ginger slices. Pour rice wine and fish sauce over fish.

When the water is boiling, remove the lid from the wok and position the plate containing the salmon and seasonings on top of the chopsticks. Replace the lid and cook 7 to 8 minutes, or until the salmon just turns opaque and begins to flake.

Two to three minutes before the salmon is done steaming, heat the peanut oil in a small skillet over high heat. When the oil is very hot, add the garlic and cook until browned. Discard the garlic, but do not turn off the heat until you use the oil; it must be very hot to sear the fish properly.

When the salmon is cooked, transfer to a warm plate. Place green onion strips on top of the fish and immediately pour hot oil over the fish and onions. Garnish with cilantro sprigs and serve immediately.

Serves 2 as an entrée, 4 as an appetizer

Cold-Smoked Salmon with
Corn Bread Pudding, Shiitake Relish, and Fried Basil

Etta's Seafood, Seattle, Washington

THIS IS ONE OF THE BEST renditions of salmon in town. It's chef/owner Tom Douglas's signature dish from Etta's Seafood, located just north of the Pike Place Public Market.

> *$1/4$ cup sugar*
> *1 tablespoon kosher salt*
> *1 teaspoon minced fresh thyme*
> *2 tablespoons sweet paprika*
> *$2^1/4$ teaspoons coarsely ground black pepper*
> *$1^1/2$ pounds salmon fillets, skin and bones removed, rinsed, drained, patted dry,*
> *   and cut into 4 (6-ounce) pieces*
> *2 teaspoons butter*
> *1 tablespoon olive oil*
> *30 fresh basil leaves*
> *Corn Bread Pudding (recipe follows)*
> *Shiitake Relish (recipe follows)*
> *$1/2$ lemon, cut into 4 wedges, for garnish*

In a small bowl, combine the sugar, salt, thyme, paprika, and black pepper. Pat the spice mixture over both sides of the salmon fillets. Wrap the fillets in plastic wrap and refrigerate 3 to 6 hours.

Rinse the fillets under cold running water, then pat dry with paper towels. Put the fillets on a plate, do not cover, and place in the refrigerator overnight to dry.

Prepare an electric smoker (see Note) according to the manufacturer's instructions and cold-smoke the salmon fillets at 80°F to 100°F for 1 hour. Remove from the smoker and refrigerate until ready to use.

Ten minutes before cooking, preheat oven to 450°F. Lightly coat a baking sheet with oil or nonstick cooking spray, and set aside.

Heat a large skillet over medium-high heat. Add butter and, when melted, add the salmon fillets, flesh side down. Cook 2 minutes, or until lightly browned. Turn and cook 2 minutes more, or until the skin is lightly browned. Place the salmon on baking sheet, skin side down, and bake in the oven for 4 to 5 minutes, or until salmon is just opaque.

Meanwhile, heat the olive oil in a small skillet over medium-high heat. When the pan is very hot, add the basil leaves and cook 30 seconds to 1 minute, or until the basil turns bright green. Drain the basil leaves on several layers of paper towels and reserve.

To serve, spoon warm Corn Bread Pudding into the center of warmed individual plates. Top with salmon, placing it slightly to one side. Spoon Shiitake Relish over salmon fillets and sprinkle with fried basil leaves. Garnish with lemon slices and serve immediately.

Serves 4

Note: *Cold-smoking can be a tricky technique. At Etta's, they use a commercial smoker; many home smokers simply are not capable of duplicating the results. As an alternative, the salmon may be taken to a local smoke-house, such as Portlock or Jensen's in Seattle, and cold-smoked there. A simpler alternative is to pat the salmon fillets with the spice rub, wrap and refrigerate the fillets several hours or overnight, rinse and pat dry, then proceed with the recipe at the paragraph beginning "Ten minutes before cooking." The result will be different because there will be no smoky flavor, but it will still be delicious.*

(subrecipes follow)

Corn Bread Pudding

5 cups 1-inch cubes corn bread (recipe follows)

1 tablespoon butter plus extra to butter pan

1 onion, cut into 1/8-inch-thick slices

3 cups heavy whipping cream

6 eggs

1 1/2 cups grated dry Monterey Jack cheese

1 1/2 tablespoons mixed chopped fresh parsley, chives, and thyme or other herbs

2 teaspoons salt

1 teaspoon freshly ground black pepper

Preheat oven to 375°F. Grease a deep 12 x 9-inch baking pan or a 13 x 9-inch baking pan with butter.

Fill baking pan with corn bread cubes. Heat the remaining 1 tablespoon butter in a large skillet over medium-low to medium heat and cook the onion 20 minutes, or until very soft and golden brown. Recipe may be prepared up to this point 1 day in advance.

One hour before serving, whisk the whipping cream and eggs until well blended. Stir in the cooked onion, Monterey Jack cheese, herbs, salt, and pepper. Pour the cream mixture over the corn bread in the pan. Bake 45 minutes, or until the pudding is set, the top is golden, and a knife blade inserted into the center comes out clean.

Corn Bread

1 cup all-purpose flour
2 teaspoons baking powder
1 teaspoon salt
3/4 cup cornmeal
1/2 cup grated pepper Jack cheese
2 eggs
1 cup milk
1 tablespoon honey
4 tablespoons butter, melted

Preheat oven to 425°F. Generously grease a 9 x 9-inch baking pan.

Sift the flour, baking powder, and salt together into a large mixing bowl. Add the cornmeal and cheese and mix well.

FUN FACT

Northwest natives often left their salmon in the smokehouse for two weeks, which resulted in a dark brown, very smoky salmon. They also took smoked salmon, dried and seasoned it, and cut it into thin strips to make "squaw candy," something similar to beef jerky that was eaten between meals as a snack. "Squaw candy" is a popular food for modern-day hikers and campers.

In a small mixing bowl, whisk together the eggs, milk, and honey. Make a well in the center of the dry ingredients and add the wet ingredients, stirring just to combine. Stir in melted butter. Pour batter into baking pan and bake 20 to 25 minutes, or until the top is golden brown and a toothpick inserted into the center comes out clean. The corn bread may be made up to 3 days in advance, and allowed to dry slightly before making the pudding.

Shiitake Relish

3/4 pound fresh shiitake mushrooms
2 to 3 tablespoons olive oil
Salt and freshly ground black pepper
2 tablespoons minced shallots
2 teaspoons minced garlic
2 tablespoons mixed chopped fresh thyme, rosemary, sage, oregano, and parsley
1 tablespoon balsamic vinegar
1 1/2 teaspoons freshly squeezed lemon juice
2 tablespoons extra virgin olive oil

Preheat grill.

Remove stems from the mushrooms and discard. Wipe the mushroom caps with damp paper towels to remove surface dirt. Brush the caps lightly with 1 to 2 tablespoons of the olive oil and place on the grill. Grill on both sides until browned and cooked through, about 2 to 3 minutes on each side. Cut the mushrooms into very thin strips, place in a bowl, season lightly with salt and pepper, and reserve.

Heat the remaining 1 tablespoon olive oil in a skillet over low heat. Add the shallots and garlic and sweat 3 to 4 minutes, or until soft, stirring occasionally. Do not allow to brown. Allow to cool slightly, then add the shallots to the mushrooms. Stir in the fresh herb mixture.

In a small mixing bowl, whisk together the balsamic vinegar, lemon juice, and extra virgin olive oil. Pour over the mushroom mixture and toss gently. Season to taste with salt and pepper. Shiitake Relish is best served the same day it is made.

Makes 1 1/2 cups

Alaskan Salmon with Warm Blackberry and Shallot Compote

McCormick & Schmick's, Seattle, Washington

THIS IS THE PERFECT DISH to make at the height of summer, when blackberries are in their prime and Alaskan sockeye salmon are running strong.

> *3 to 4 shallots, peeled*
> *2 tablespoons olive oil*
> *1/4 cup sugar*
> *2 cups fresh blackberries, gently rinsed, drained, and patted dry*
> *1/4 cup raspberry vinegar*
> *1/4 cup all-purpose flour*
> *1 tablespoon minced fresh chervil*
> *1 tablespoon minced fresh parsley*
> *Pinch of salt*
> *Pinch of freshly ground black pepper*
> *1 1/2 pounds salmon fillets, skin and bones removed, rinsed, drained, patted dry,*
>   *and cut into 4 (6-ounce) pieces*

Preheat oven to 400°F.

In a mixing bowl, toss the shallots, 1 tablespoon of the olive oil, and the sugar. Spread in a baking pan and cook 10 to 15 minutes, or until the shallots are lightly browned and soft. Remove from the oven and spoon shallots and syrup into a nonreactive mixing bowl with a lid. Add the blackberries and raspberry vinegar and toss gently to mix the ingredients, being careful not to break up the berries. Cover the bowl and set aside.

Place a nonstick skillet large enough to hold the salmon fillets without crowding over medium heat. When the pan is hot, add the remaining 1 tablespoon olive oil. While oil is heating, mix together the flour, chervil, parsley, salt, and pepper on a plate or a piece of waxed paper. Pat both sides of the salmon fillets in the flour mixture, then shake off the excess.

When the oil is hot, add the salmon fillets and cook 3 to 5 minutes. Turn and cook 3 to 5 minutes more, or until the fish just turns opaque.

To serve, transfer the salmon fillets to individual plates and spoon compote over the top of the fish.

Serves 4

Spicy Smoked Salmon with Wasabi Dipping Sauce

BY CURING a side of salmon overnight in a marinade brimming with freshly ground spices and a touch of liquid smoke, then cooking the fish in a low oven, the pink flesh becomes meltingly tender and flavorful, with a taste similar to smoked salmon.

1 tablespoon Salmon Spice Mix (recipe follows)
1 tablespoon soy sauce
1 tablespoon mirin
1 tablespoon sake
1 tablespoon unseasoned rice vinegar
1 tablespoon canola oil or sesame oil
1 tablespoon maple syrup
1 tablespoon liquid smoke
Pinch of salt
Pinch of freshly ground black pepper
Pinch of crushed red pepper flakes

(continued)

1 side of salmon, filleted and bones removed, with skin (about 2¹/₂ pounds)
Freshly ground white pepper
Wasabi Dipping Sauce (recipe follows)

Place the Salmon Spice Mix, soy sauce, mirin, sake, rice vinegar, canola oil, maple syrup, liquid smoke, salt, black pepper, and red pepper flakes in a small nonreactive bowl with a lid and mix until well blended.

Place a piece of plastic wrap lengthwise on a baking sheet, allowing 8 inches of extra wrap at each end to cover the salmon. Place the salmon on plastic wrap, skin side down. Spoon half the marinade over the salmon and rub it into the flesh. Turn the salmon over and cover completely with plastic wrap. Place the salmon and leftover marinade in refrigerator overnight.

One hour before cooking, remove the salmon and the remaining marinade from the refrigerator and let sit at room temperature. Ten minutes before cooking, preheat the oven to 275°F. Place a rack large enough to hold the fish on a baking sheet and spray the rack with nonstick cooking spray.

When the oven is hot, place the salmon on the rack, skin side down. Pour half of the remaining marinade over the salmon, patting it gently.

Place the baking sheet on the top rack of oven and roast the salmon for 15 minutes. Remove the

---

FUN FACT

The Native Americans' favorite way to cook salmon was to place an opened, cleaned fish between two tree branches fastened with small lateral twigs to hold the fish spread open before the fire. They also liked to plank their salmon on driftwood or sandwich it between alder or cedar wood, which was then stacked around a crackling fire. Clams, mussels, oysters, and barnacles were cooked in a similar fashion (they were never eaten raw). They were then strung on buckskin or cedar bark for winter storage.

salmon from oven and cover with the remaining marinade. Return salmon to the oven for 30 to 45 minutes more, or until opaque throughout and golden brown in color.

To serve, remove the skin (if desired), and place the fish on a serving platter. Sprinkle lightly with pepper and pass the Wasabi Dipping Sauce at the table.

Serves 6 to 8 as an entrée, 12 as an appetizer

Salmon Spice Mix

1 whole star anise
1 tablespoon whole coriander seeds
4 whole allspice berries
1 (3-inch) stick cinnamon, broken into several pieces

Place all of the ingredients in a spice mill or small, clean electric coffee grinder and process until very finely ground. Pour the spices into a small nonreactive bowl or jar with a lid, cover, and set aside.

Wasabi Dipping Sauce

1 tablespoon wasabi powder
1 tablespoon soy sauce
1 tablespoon water
2 tablespoons honey mustard

Stir together all of the ingredients in a small nonreactive bowl. Allow to sit at room temperature at least 10 minutes to allow the flavors to blend, or cover and refrigerate until use.

Makes about 1/4 cup

Baked Salmon with Tarragon Pesto

TARRAGON IS MY FAVORITE HERB, and pesto is such a popular sauce that I decided to merge the two in this savory topping for sturdy salmon fillets.

>1 1/2 *pounds salmon fillets, bones removed, rinsed, drained, patted dry,*
> *and cut into 4 (6-ounce) pieces*
>1/2 *cup lightly packed fresh tarragon leaves, minced, plus tarragon sprigs for garnish*
>6 *tablespoons fine, unseasoned dry bread crumbs (see page 127)*
>3 *tablespoons olive oil*
>1 1/2 *tablespoons tarragon vinegar or white wine vinegar*
>2 *cloves garlic, minced*
>1/4 *teaspoon salt*
>1/8 *teaspoon crushed red pepper flakes*
>*Lemon wedges, for garnish*

Preheat oven to 400°F. Lightly coat a baking sheet with oil or nonstick cooking spray. Place the fish fillets on the baking sheet, skin side down, evenly spaced, without crowding. Set aside while preparing the pesto.

In a small bowl, mix the minced tarragon, bread crumbs, olive oil, vinegar, garlic, salt, and red pepper flakes. Spread evenly over the tops of the salmon fillets, pressing down with the back of a spoon to help the topping adhere to the fish.

Place the fish in the oven and cook 8 to 12 minutes, depending on the thickness of the fillets, until the fish just turns opaque.

To serve, divide the fillets among individual plates and garnish with lemon wedges and tarragon sprigs.

Serves 4

Baked Whole Salmon with Vietnamese Dipping Sauce

Saigon Restaurant, Pike Place Public Market

THERE'S SOMETHING CEREMONIAL and celebratory about serving a whole baked fish, and this classic Vietnamese interpretation from the Market's very own Saigon Restaurant is one of the easiest and best.

> *¹/₂ teaspoon salt*
> *¹/₄ teaspoon freshly ground white pepper*
> *2 tablespoons low-sodium soy sauce*
> *2 tablespoons dry white wine or chicken broth*
> *1 4-pound salmon, gutted*
> *4 cloves garlic, thinly sliced*
> *2 quarter-size slices gingerroot, smashed with the flat part of a knife blade
>   and julienned*
> *6 to 8 green onions, white part julienned, green part cut into ¹/₄-inch slices
>   and reserved*
> *3 tablespoons peanut oil or sesame oil*
> *Vietnamese Dipping Sauce (recipe follows)*

Place a sheet of aluminum foil lengthwise across a baking sheet, extending the foil 8 to 10 inches beyond the ends of the sheet. Place a second sheet of foil widthwise across the baking sheet, again allowing 8 to 10 inches of excess foil on each side. Set aside.

In a small mixing bowl or glass jar with a lid, combine the salt, white pepper, soy sauce, and white wine to make the seasoning mix. Stir or shake well to combine and set aside.

Rinse the fish under cold running water, being especially careful to remove any blood remaining in the stomach cavity. Pat dry inside and out with paper towels. Place the fish on the foil-lined baking sheet.

With a sharp knife, make 6 to 8 diagonal scores from top to bottom on both sides of the fish, about $1/4$ inch deep. Rub seasoning mix into the sides of the fish and into the stomach cavity. Stuff cuts with garlic, ginger, and green onion julienne. Sprinkle fish with any remaining garlic, ginger, and green onion julienne. Carefully fold sides of foil over fish to seal fish tightly. Let foil-wrapped fish sit at room temperature for 20 minutes.

Ten minutes before you are ready to cook, preheat the oven to 400°F. Place the baking sheet in the center of the oven and bake for 20 minutes, or until the flesh is firm and rosy, but still juicy at the base of the cuts. Remove from the oven and fold back top of the foil to expose the fish. Return the fish to the oven and bake an additional 10 minutes, or until the fish just flakes. Remove the fish from the foil and transfer to a large serving platter.

Heat the peanut oil in a small skillet over medium-high heat. Add the reserved green onion slices and cook for 5 to 10 seconds, stirring continuously. Remove the skillet from the heat and pour the flavored oil over the fish.

Serve the whole fish at the table with dipping sauce.

Serves 4

Vietnamese Dipping Sauce

$^1/_4$ cup Vietnamese fish sauce (nuoc nam)
1 clove garlic, crushed
1 Thai chile, seeded and minced
2 teaspoons sugar
1 teaspoon freshly squeezed lemon juice

Place all the ingredients in a small bowl and stir until the sugar dissolves. Cover and set aside if using immediately, or refrigerate until ready to use.

Makes about $^1/_4$ cup

Note: *The technique of using a hot seasoned oil over steamed or baked fish is known as flavor smoothing and helps force the flavors of the seasoning into the fish. You can vary the flavor of the seasoned oil by substituting minced garlic, chopped fresh basil leaves, or chopped cilantro.*

Smoked Salmon Pasta Salad

Totem Smokehouse, Pike Place Public Market

RICH IN TEXTURE, color, and flavor, this easy pasta salad would be great for a summer picnic or to take to a potluck supper.

> *1 (9-ounce) package fresh cheese tortellini or 1/2 pound dry cheese tortellini*
> *1/4 cup chopped celery*
> *1/4 cup chopped red bell pepper*
> *1 (8 3/4-ounce) can garbanzo beans, drained*
> *1 (2 1/2-ounce) can sliced black olives, drained*
> *1 (6 1/2-ounce) jar marinated artichoke hearts, drained of oil and chopped*
> *2 tablespoons chopped fresh basil*
> *Dressing (recipe follows)*
> *8 ounces hot-smoked salmon, skin and bones removed, crumbled*
> *Freshly ground black pepper*
> *Freshly grated Parmesan cheese*

Cook the tortellini according to the package instructions. Rinse under cold running water, drain well, and pour into a large mixing bowl. Add the celery, red bell pepper, garbanzo beans, olives, artichoke hearts, basil, and Dressing and toss to mix. Gently stir the smoked salmon into the pasta salad.

To serve, divide the salad among individual plates and sprinkle with pepper and Parmesan cheese.

Serves 4

SALMON WINES

Salmon is an oily fish with fairly strong flavors. No matter the species, salmon has enough oil, body, and texture to stand up to a wide array of wines, everything from a full-bodied white (such as a Chardonnay) to a lighter, less overbearing red (such as Pinot Noir).

Wild salmon, in particular, is a rich, meaty fish with mul-tiple dimensions of flavor described as "nutty," "woodsy," and "game-like," flavors that pair well with Pinot Noir. Pinot Noir, characterized by delicacy and subtlety in both flavor and texture, ranges from light and fruity when young, to full-flavored and complex as it ages.

Other wines, such as Melon, Sauvignon Blanc (sometimes referred to as Fumé Blanc), and Pinot Gris (a.k.a. Pinot Grigio), work well with salmon.

Smoked salmon is tough to pair with wine for two main reasons. The saltiness and smokiness tend to dull most wines, while the fatty texture and inherent fishiness of the salmon make many wines develop an off flavor. That is probably the reason smoked salmon is often paired with chilled vodka (since the liquor has an almost neutral taste) or Champagne or sparkling wines (since the bubbles cut through the fattiness of the fish and don't compete with the smoke). Smoked salmon appetizers, in which the salmon is layered atop puff pastry or a potato pancake and dolloped with sour cream or crème fraîche and snipped chives, are more forgiving. They are easily served with chilled white wines, such as Sauvignon, Chenin, or Pinot Blanc, for a successful pairing.

Dressing

1/2 cup red wine vinegar
1/4 cup olive oil
1 tablespoon chopped red onion
1 1/2 teaspoons sugar
1 teaspoon dry mustard
1 teaspoon dried basil, crumbled
1/2 teaspoon Dijon mustard
1/2 teaspoon dried oregano, crumbled
2 cloves garlic, crushed

In a small mixing bowl, whisk together all of the ingredients except the garlic until the sugar is dissolved. Add the garlic, cover the bowl, and place in the refrigerator at least 2 hours, and preferably overnight, to allow the flavors to blend. Remove the crushed garlic cloves before adding the dressing to the pasta salad.

Makes 3/4 cup

Smoked Salmon
Dutch Baby with Dill Sauce

DUTCH BABIES are puffy pancakes cooked in a skillet in the oven. Although they are usually served with a sweet lemon sauce, I have turned the dish into a savory one with the addition of smoked salmon and sautéed vegetables. Do not open the oven door while baking, which will cause the pancake to fall!

> 1 tablespoon olive oil
> 1/2 white or yellow onion, chopped
> 1/2 red bell pepper, chopped
> 1 tablespoon butter
> 3/4 cup lowfat milk
> 1/3 cup all-purpose flour
> Pinch of freshly ground white pepper
> 4 eggs or 1 cup egg substitute
> 1 1/2 teaspoons ground sweet paprika
> 1 (3-ounce) package thinly sliced cold-smoked salmon, such as Nova style or lox
> Dill Sauce (recipe follows)

Preheat oven to 400°F.

Heat the olive oil in a medium skillet over medium-high heat. Add the onion and red bell pepper and cook until the vegetables are tender, about 5 to 7 minutes, stirring often. Remove from heat and set aside.

Melt the butter in a large, nonstick, ovenproof skillet in the oven until sizzling. Wrap the handle of the skillet with aluminum foil if it is not ovenproof and check the skillet frequently to make sure the butter doesn't burn.

(continued)

Meanwhile, add the milk, flour, and white pepper to a food processor or blender and pulse until blended. Add the eggs and process just until blended.

Remove the skillet from the oven and transfer the reserved vegetables to the skillet, distributing evenly. Immediately pour in the egg batter. Bake, uncovered, in the center of the oven until the Dutch baby is puffed and lightly browned, about 12 to 15 minutes.

Remove the pan from the oven, sprinkle evenly with paprika, and arrange the salmon slices evenly over the top of the pancake. Cut into 8 wedges and serve immediately, or allow to come to room temperature before serving.

To serve, place 2 wedges on each plate and place a dollop of Dill Sauce beside the wedges.

Serves 4 as an appetizer

Dill Sauce

1/4 cup plain lowfat yogurt
1/4 cup lowfat sour cream
1 tablespoon fresh snipped dill, or 1 teaspoon dried dill, crumbled
Tabasco sauce
Salt

Place the yogurt, sour cream, and dill in a small mixing bowl and stir to blend. Season to taste with Tabasco and salt. Cover and refrigerate until ready to use.

Makes 1/2 cup

Scandinavian Pasta

I HAVE BEEN making this ultra-simple pasta dish for years to rave reviews from family and friends, and nobody ever guesses how easy it really is.

> *3/4 pound conchiglie (seashell), rotini (spaghetti spirals), or farfalle (butterfly or*
>   *bow-tie pasta)*
> *2 tablespoons unsalted butter, at room temperature*
> *1/4 cup fresh snipped dill, or 1 tablespoon dried dill, crumbled*
> *2 (3-ounce) packages thinly sliced cold-smoked salmon, such as Nova style or lox,*
>   *chopped*
> *Pinch of freshly ground white pepper*

Cook the pasta according to the package instructions. Drain well, reserving the pasta and 1/4 cup of the pasta cooking water.

In a large mixing bowl, combine the butter, dill, smoked salmon, and pepper and toss gently to blend. Add the reserved pasta and toss gently until ingredients are thoroughly mixed. If pasta is dry, add reserved pasta water bit by bit, stirring after each addition, until desired consistency is reached. Taste and add additional pepper, if desired.

To serve, place the pasta on a large serving platter or divide among individual bowls and serve immediately.

Serves 4

Part III

Shellfish

Alaskan Spot Prawn Wonton Salad

Anthony's Homeport, various locations throughout the Puget Sound area

THIS UNIQUE SPOT PRAWN SALAD was served at the James Beard House in New York City, where it played to rave reviews.

> 3 tablespoons vegetable oil
> 10 wonton wrappers, sliced into $1/4$-inch strips
> 1 tablespoon butter
> 2 cloves garlic, cut in half
> $3/4$ pound Alaskan spot prawns, shelled and deveined
> 2 cups thinly sliced Napa cabbage plus 4 to 8 large, attractive outer leaves
> 1 cup thinly sliced romaine lettuce
> $1/4$ cup shredded carrot
> 3 tablespoons chopped cilantro plus extra cilantro sprigs, for garnish
> $1/2$ cup finely sliced Chinese pea pods or sugar snap peas
> 2 tablespoons thinly sliced green onions
> $1/2$ cup bean sprouts, rinsed, drained, and patted dry
> 2 teaspoons black sesame seeds
> 1 cup Rice Vinegar Dressing (recipe follows)
> Pickled ginger, for garnish

In a large skillet, heat the vegetable oil over medium-high heat. When the oil is very hot, add about a third of the wonton strips. Fry 2 to 3 minutes, or until golden brown, turning once, then drain on paper towels. Repeat in batches until all strips are fried, adding more oil if necessary.

Heat a large nonstick skillet over medium heat. When pan is hot, add butter. When butter is melted, add garlic and cook 1 minute, stirring continuously. Remove garlic, add prawns, and cook 2 minutes. Turn prawns and cook 2 minutes more, or until prawns just turn pink. Place prawns in a large mixing bowl and add wonton strips, sliced Napa cabbage, romaine lettuce, carrot, chopped cilantro, Chinese pea pods, green onions, bean sprouts, black sesame seeds, and Rice Vinegar Dressing. Toss salad.

Line individual plates with Napa cabbage leaves and spoon salad into leaves. Garnish with cilantro sprigs and pickled ginger.

Serves 4

Rice Vinegar Dressing

1/2 cup unseasoned rice vinegar
1/2 cup vegetable oil
3 tablespoons sugar
1 1/2 tablespoons soy sauce
1 tablespoon toasted sesame oil
1 tablespoon freshly squeezed lime juice
1/8 teaspoon dry mustard

Whisk together all of the ingredients in a large mixing bowl. Use immediately, or cover and refrigerate for up to 1 week.

Makes about 1 cup

Shrimp 'n' Vegetable Quiche

Lowell's Restaurant & Bar, Pike Place Public Market

SERVED WITH a tossed green salad and a glass of sparkling wine or cider, this seafood pie makes a special lunch, weekend brunch, or light dinner entrée.

> *1 prepared 9-inch pie shell, unbaked*
> *1 teaspoon vegetable oil*
> *1 cup assorted mixed chopped vegetables (such as red bell pepper, red onion, zucchini,*
>   *yellow squash, and broccoli florets)*
> *2 cloves garlic, minced*
> *2 tablespoons snipped fresh dill, or 2 teaspoons dried dill, crumbled*
> *1/2 pound pink (bay or salad) shrimp, rinsed and patted very dry*
> *1/4 cup grated Cheddar cheese*
> *1/4 cup grated provolone cheese*
> *3 eggs*
> *3/4 cup half-and-half*
> *1/8 teaspoon salt*
> *1/4 teaspoon freshly ground white pepper*

Preheat oven to 400°F. Bake the pie crust 8 to 10 minutes, or until pale golden in color. Transfer to a rack while preparing the rest of the recipe. Decrease the oven temperature to 325°F.

Heat the vegetable oil in a medium nonstick skillet over medium heat. Add the vegetables and cook 5 to 7 minutes, stirring often, or until the vegetables are tender-crisp. Add the garlic and dill and stir to blend. Remove the pan from the heat and add the shrimp, stirring well.

Spread shrimp and vegetables evenly over bottom of pie crust and sprinkle with Cheddar and provolone cheeses. In a medium bowl, whisk together eggs, half-and-half, and salt and pepper. Carefully pour egg mixture over shrimp and vegetables. Using the back of a spoon, gently press the vegetables, shrimp, and cheese to below the level of the eggs.

Place quiche on a rack in the center of the oven and bake 40 to 50 minutes, or until a knife inserted into center of quiche comes out clean. Remove from oven and allow to cool at least 20 minutes before cutting and serving.

Serves 4 as an entrée, 8 as an appetizer

FUN FACT

A sea fungus called *Phaffia* synthesizes pink pigment, which no other organism is known to do. It's what makes the flesh of shrimp and salmon turn pink.

Vietnamese Shrimp Rolls with Hoisin Dipping Sauce

THESE HEALTHY SHRIMP rolls epitomize Vietnamese cuisine, which is characterized by the use of raw vegetables and light sauces.

6 tablespoons freshly squeezed lime juice

2 tablespoons Vietnamese fish sauce (nuoc nam)

4 cloves garlic, minced

1/4 teaspoon crushed red pepper flakes

1 1/2 pounds pink (bay or salad) shrimp, rinsed, drained, and patted dry

16 pieces rice paper

16 soft lettuce leaves, such as Bibb, red or green leaf, or iceberg

2 cups bean sprouts, rinsed, drained, and patted dry

2 cups shredded carrots

1/2 cup crushed unsalted peanuts

4 green onions, roots and tips removed, cut into 1/8-inch rounds

Fresh basil leaves or fresh mint leaves

Hoisin Dipping Sauce (recipe follows)

In a medium mixing bowl, stir together the lime juice, fish sauce, garlic, and red pepper flakes. Add the shrimp and toss well to coat. Cover the bowl and refrigerate.

Take out 2 large plates and pour 1/4 inch warm water into one of them. Place 1 piece of rice paper in the water and soak for 30 seconds to 1 minute, or until pliable. Do not allow to soak too long or the rice paper will tear. Remove the rice paper to a dry plate, then repeat the process with the remaining rice paper sheets.

Place lettuce leaves around the perimeter of a large serving platter. Put the shrimp in a serving bowl and place in the center of the platter. Put the bean sprouts, carrots, peanuts, green onions, and basil leaves in separate piles around the shrimp.

To serve, place rice paper, prepared platter, and Hoisin Dipping Sauce on the table and allow everyone to make their own shrimp rolls by lining a piece of rice paper with a lettuce leaf and adding vegetables, shrimp, peanuts, and basil leaves and folding or rolling to close. The shrimp rolls can then be dipped in the sauce.

Serves 4 as an entrée, 8 as an appetizer

Hoisin Dipping Sauce

6 tablespoons hoisin sauce
6 tablespoons seasoned rice vinegar
2 tablespoons soy sauce or low-sodium soy sauce

In a small mixing bowl, stir together the hoisin sauce, seasoned rice vinegar, and soy sauce. If not using immediately, cover and refrigerate.

Makes about 3/4 cup

ALASKAN SPOT PRAWN AND BAY SHRIMP WINES

Alaskan spot prawns, with their delicate, slightly sweet taste and firm texture, work well with medium-dry to dry Riesling, Chenin Blanc, Sémillon, Sauvignon Blanc, and Muscat Canelli. "Spots" also often pair advantageously with beer, particularly lighter-style Northwest microbrews. Spanish dry Fino Sherry paired with spicy/tomatoey/garlicky shrimp dishes has kept the Iberians happy for hundreds of years. Fruity reds (such as Zinfandel and Merlot) pair advantageously with Mediterranean shrimp dishes and hearty shrimp soups and stews.

Northwest Clambake in the Oven

THIS CLAMBAKE can be prepared in your own kitchen with results as tasty as if it had been cooked in the great outdoors.

> 2 large soft lettuce leaves, such as Bibb, green leaf, or iceberg
> 1 halibut fillet, about 3 ounces, skin and bones removed, rinsed, drained,
>   and patted dry
> 6 clams, purged and shells scrubbed
> 6 mussels, scrubbed and debearded just before cooking
> 3 Alaskan spot prawns, cut down the back with scissors and vein extracted
> 2 to 3 small new potatoes, about 1 1/2 inches in diameter, cut in half
> 1 ear corn, husk removed and broken or cut into thirds
> 6 snow peas, strings removed
> 1 small yellow squash or zucchini, ends removed and cut into 1/2-inch rounds
> 1 clove garlic, minced
> Fresh rosemary, thyme, or tarragon sprigs
> 1/4 cup clam juice, fish stock, or chicken stock

Preheat oven to 350°F.

Cut two 24-inch lengths of aluminum foil and place on a flat surface in a cross-shaped pattern. Place the lettuce leaves in the center of the foil and top with the halibut fillet, then place the clams, mussels, and spot prawns on top. Place the potatoes, corn, snow peas, and yellow squash around the halibut, then pull up sides of the foil around the vegetables to form a bowl shape. Sprinkle the garlic over the seafood and vegetables, place the herb sprigs on top of the seafood, then drizzle clam juice over all.

(continued)

CLAM WINES

Clams possess a slightly musky, sweet taste and a slightly chewy, yet pleasant texture. Young, lean white wines such as Sémillon, Sémillon-Chardonnay, Chardonnay (lean, acidic styles that are not heavily oaked or buttery), Sauvignon Blanc, Chenin Blanc, Sauvignon Blanc–Sémillon blends, Pinot Gris, Melon, Riesling, and Dry Riesling all pair well with the shellfish's unique taste and texture. Of course, much depends on the sauce served with the bivalves. If serving clams in a spicy tomato-based sauce, some fruity red wines, such as Merlot or Zinfandel, make a good match. When cooking clams with Asian-style treatments, sake or Asian beer may make a better partner.

Bring the long sides of foil up until they meet in the middle and secure tightly. Fold the remaining ends to seal tightly. Place the packet on a baking sheet and bake 1 hour.

To serve, place the packet on an individual plate and unfold or cut open the foil at the table for an informal presentation. Alternately, unfold the foil in the kitchen, transfer contents of the packet to a plate, and discard the foil.

Serves 1

FUN FACT

"The Nisqually and other coast-dwelling tribes prepared clam chowders in winter months, using dried, powdered clams for a base. In one traditional recipe, clams were pulverized, then simmered in bentwood boxes or baskets filled with hot water. Wild onions and dried seaweed helped season the chowder; only with the arrival of European settlers and their crops did Native Americans add potatoes, celery, carrots, salt, pepper, and a particular favorite—bacon fat—to their geoduck chowders and stews."

—Field Guide to the Geoduck

Smoky Clam Chowder

Jack's Fish Spot, Pike Place Public Market

THE ADDITION of hard-cooked smoked salmon, also known as salmon jerky, gives this rendition of clam chowder a hearty flavor and a real Northwest flair.

> *2 tablespoons butter*
> *1 1/2 cups 1/2-inch cubes boiling potatoes*
> *1/2 cup chopped celery*
> *1/2 cup chopped onion*
> *1 (8-ounce) bottle clam juice*
> *2 cups milk*
> *Pinch of dried thyme, crumbled*
> *Pinch of crushed red pepper flakes*
> *2 (6.5-ounce) cans chopped clams, with juice*
> *1 cup heavy whipping cream*
> *2 to 3 tablespoons diced hard-smoked salmon*
> *Salt and freshly ground black pepper*

Melt the butter in a large saucepan over medium heat and add the potatoes, celery, and onion. Cook 5 minutes, stirring occasionally, or until the vegetables are tender-crisp.

Add clam juice, milk, thyme, and red pepper flakes. Stir well and bring to a simmer. Simmer gently 10 minutes, stirring occasionally, until potatoes are tender. Add the clams, whipping cream, and smoked salmon, and stir well. Cook several minutes more, or until the mixture is warmed through. Season to taste with salt and pepper.

Ladle the clam chowder into soup bowls and serve right away.

Serves 4

Geoduck Fritters

Pure Food Fish, Pike Place Public Market

THESE LIGHT, melt-in-your-mouth fritters are full of the unmistakable flavor of the geoduck clam.

> 1 cup all-purpose flour
> 1 teaspoon baking powder
> $1/2$ teaspoon salt
> $1/8$ teaspoon freshly ground black pepper
> Dash of ground nutmeg
> $1/3$ cup clam juice
> 2 eggs, beaten
> $1/3$ cup milk
> 2 teaspoons butter, melted
> 1 geoduck, cleaned and diced (see note)
> Vegetable oil, for frying
> Lemon wedges, for garnish

Preheat oven to 200°F. Line a baking sheet with paper towels and set aside.

Sift the flour, baking powder, salt, pepper, and nutmeg into a mixing bowl. Add the clam juice, eggs, and milk and beat thoroughly with a wire whisk. Fold in the butter and geoduck.

Fill a large saucepan or wok halfway with vegetable oil and heat to 375°F. Very carefully, drop large spoonfuls of batter into the hot oil and cook 3 to 4 minutes, turning once, or until the fritters are golden on both sides. Drain on paper towels, then transfer the fritters to the prepared baking sheet and place in the oven to keep warm. Repeat the procedure with the remaining batter.

To serve, divide the fritters among individual plates and serve immediately.

Serves 4

Note: *Geoducks can be tricky (and messy) to clean. Any good fishmonger will be glad to clean the giant clam as you desire.*

Cold Crab Cakes with Fresh Chive Aïoli

Rover's, Seattle, Washington

TAKING HIS INSPIRATION from cold crab salad and what was available in his larder, Thierry Rautureau, chef/owner of Rover's, prepared several hundred of these crab cakes for a fund-raiser.

> *¹/₂ pound snow peas, strings removed*
> *1 red bell pepper, stemmed, seeded, and diced*
> *1 yellow bell pepper, stemmed, seeded, and diced*
> *3 tablespoons ocean salad (optional; see note on page 92)*
> *2 tablespoons minced shallots*
> *10 ounces (2 cups) fresh Dungeness crabmeat, picked over for shells and cartilage*
> *2 egg yolks*
> *2 cloves garlic, minced*
> *1¹/₂ teaspoons Dijon mustard*
> *1¹/₂ teaspoons prepared horseradish*
> *6 tablespoons extra virgin olive oil*
> *1 tablespoon red wine vinegar*
> *1 tablespoon minced fresh chives*
> *Salt and freshly ground white pepper*
> *Mesclun (gourmet salad mix), for garnish*

In a medium saucepan, bring enough water to cover snow peas to a boil, add snow peas, and cook 1 to 2 minutes. Drain and rinse with cold water to stop the cooking process. Drain again, pat dry, and cut vertically into ¹/₈-inch strips. Place in a large mixing bowl along with the red bell pepper, yellow bell pepper, ocean salad, shallots, and crabmeat. Cover the bowl and refrigerate.

To make aïoli, whisk the egg yolks, garlic, mustard, and horseradish until thoroughly blended. Add the olive oil in a thin stream, whisking continuously until the mixture emulsifies. Add vinegar and chives, and season to taste with salt and pepper.

Take out the crab mixture, add aïoli, and toss thoroughly but gently.

To serve, place a 2- or 3-inch aluminum ring on a plate and spoon the crabmeat mixture into the ring, packing loosely and leveling off the top. Prepare 1 crab cake per plate if serving as an appetizer, 2 cakes if serving as an entrée. Carefully remove the ring and repeat with the remaining crabmeat. Garnish the plate with a handful of mesclun.

CRAB WINES

The meat of Dungeness crabs (or "Dungies") is sweet, delicate, and buttery rich. Creamy white, large of flake, and firm in texture, it is more akin to lobster than other types of crab. Wines that pair well with the delicate, yet distinctive flavor of Dungeness crab include Dry Riesling, Chenin Blanc, Sémillon, and Sauvignon Blanc (sometimes referred to as Fumé Blanc). Fino Sherries, which are very dry, astringent wines with a distinctive nose, are also unusual and appropriate matches for crab.

Serves 4 as an entrée, 8 as an appetizer

Note: *Recent concerns about salmonella poisoning have called into question the use of raw eggs in food preparation. I would encourage the use of the freshest eggs available and a thorough washing and drying of the eggs before use. Individuals with chronic or autoimmune diseases should be informed of the uncooked eggs before eating this dish.*

Hood Canal Crab Cakes with Honey-Yogurt Salsa

THIS RECIPE comes from good friends Doug and Sue Ethridge, who serve these spicy cakes family style at the table, along with the honey-yogurt salsa and a big salad for accompaniment.

> *1/2 cup chunky hot salsa*
>
> *1/2 cup nonfat yogurt or nonfat sour cream*
>
> *1 1/2 teaspoons honey*
>
> *1 1/2 pounds (4 1/2 cups) fresh Dungeness crabmeat, picked over for shells and cartilage*
>
> *1/2 cup stemmed, seeded, and diced red bell pepper*
>
> *1/2 cup diced yellow onion*
>
> *1/2 cup cream cheese, softened*
>
> *1/2 cup mayonnaise*
>
> *1/2 teaspoon minced jalapeño pepper, or 1 tablespoon diced canned green chiles,
>   well drained*
>
> *1 teaspoon white or dark Worcestershire sauce*
>
> *1 tablespoon minced garlic chives, or 1 clove garlic, minced*
>
> *1 tablespoon minced cilantro*
>
> *1 to 2 cups Italian-style bread crumbs*

Preheat oven to 350°F. Lightly coat a large baking sheet with oil or nonstick cooking spray.

In a small mixing bowl, stir together the salsa, yogurt, and honey. Taste to be sure the honey has mellowed the heat of the salsa. If not, add a bit more honey to taste. Set aside at room temperature while preparing the crab cakes.

Drain any excess juice from the crab, then lightly toss the crab, red pepper, and onion together in a large mixing bowl. In a small mixing bowl, combine the cream cheese, mayonnaise, jalapeño, Worcestershire sauce, garlic chives, and cilantro. Add the mixture to the crabmeat and fold in gently.

Add bread crumbs a little bit at a time, stirring until the crab cakes reach patty consistency. The amount of bread crumbs you add will depend on the amount of water in the crabmeat.

Place the leftover bread crumbs on a plate or piece of waxed paper. Form the crabmeat mixture into 12 patties of equal size. Lightly coat each crab cake with bread crumbs on both sides before placing on the prepared baking sheet. When all the patties are coated, place the crab cakes in the oven and bake for 15 to 20 minutes, or until golden brown and a bit crusty at the edges.

To serve, place the crab cakes on a large serving platter and pass with the salsa at the table.

Serves 4

FUN FACT

Most female crabs have to shed their shells (molt) before mating. To help her, the male clasps her by the claw and around the sea floor they go, until he literally dances her out of her shell. It often takes hours for the female to emerge from her old shell.

Crab Soufflé Cakes with Sweet Pepper and Corn Relish

Dish D'Lish, Pike Place Public Market

TALENTED NORTHWEST CHEF, cookbook author, and Dish D'Lish co-owner Kathy Casey lightens traditional crab cakes by adding a purée of corn kernels, buttermilk, and gently beaten egg whites.

> $1/3$ cup buttermilk
> $1/2$ cup fresh or frozen corn
> 2 large eggs
> 1 teaspoon freshly squeezed lime juice
> $1/4$ teaspoon Tabasco sauce
> $1/2$ teaspoon salt
> $1/2$ teaspoon baking powder
> $1/3$ cup yellow cornmeal
> $1/4$ cup all-purpose flour
> $1/2$ pound ($1^1/2$ cups) fresh Dungeness crabmeat, picked over for shells and cartilage
> 2 green onions, finely minced
> 1 tablespoon (or more) olive oil
> Sweet Pepper and Corn Relish (recipe follows)
> $1/4$ cup sour cream, for garnish
> 4 sprigs cilantro, for garnish
> $1/2$ lime, cut into 4 wedges, for garnish

Preheat oven to 200°F.

Place the buttermilk and corn in a blender and process on high speed for 30 seconds, or until the mixture is smooth.

(continued)

Separate the eggs, reserving the whites. Place the yolks in a bowl and add the corn mixture, lime juice, Tabasco, and salt, stirring to mix well.

Sift together the baking powder, cornmeal, and flour into a medium bowl. Add to the corn mixture and mix well.

Drain any excess juice from the crab and add crabmeat to the batter. Add the green onions and stir gently.

Just before cooking, beat the egg whites until soft but not dry peaks form. Gently fold into the batter.

Heat a large nonstick skillet over medium heat until hot (until a drop of water evaporates immediately). Add 1 tablespoon olive oil and swirl to coat the pan. Spoon a heaping tablespoonful of batter into the skillet, cooking 3 or 4 cakes at a time to avoid crowding. Cook cakes about 1 1/2 minutes, or until golden; turn and continue cooking until the second side is golden and the cakes puff slightly. Continue cooking cakes in batches, adding more oil if necessary. Place cooked cakes in oven to keep warm.

Fun Fact

A king crab walks diagonally across the ocean floor. Smaller king crabs sometimes travel in domes, with as many as a thousand crabs stacked as high as 40 feet and as wide as 60. Crabs scamper down the front and up the back in a vortex, like a walking house of crab, in what biologists claim is a crab defense mechanism.

To serve the cakes, spoon 1/4 cup Sweet Pepper and Corn Relish onto the center of a warmed plate and place 3 crab cakes around the relish. Top each crab cake with a small dollop of sour cream. Garnish each plate with a sprig of cilantro and a lime wedge.

Serves 4

Sweet Pepper and Corn Relish

1 strip raw bacon, minced (or omit and increase olive oil to 1 tablespoon)

2 teaspoons olive oil

1/2 cup 1/4-inch dice red bell pepper

1/2 cup 1/4-inch dice red onion

1 teaspoon minced garlic

3/4 cup fresh or frozen corn

2 tablespoons freshly squeezed lime juice

1 1/2 tablespoons firmly packed brown sugar

1/8 teaspoon ground cayenne pepper

Pinch of crushed red pepper flakes

1/4 to 1/2 teaspoon salt

1 green onion, minced

2 tablespoons chopped cilantro

Cook the bacon in a medium nonstick skillet over medium-high heat about 2 minutes, or until crisp. Add the olive oil, red bell pepper, red onion, and garlic and cook for 2 minutes, or until the mixture just begins to soften, stirring occasionally. Add the corn and cook another 1 to 2 minutes, stirring occasionally.

Add the lime juice, brown sugar, cayenne, red pepper flakes, and salt and remove pan from heat. Let cool to room temperature, then stir in green onions and cilantro. Place the relish in a small bowl or a covered jar and refrigerate until ready to serve.

Makes 1 cup

Gingery Mussels

Sharon Kramis, cookbook author/consulting chef

THIS MUSSEL RECIPE is one of my all-time favorites, for it contains no added fats, but the broth (a flavorful combination of sake or mirin, garlic, and ginger) is the perfect complement to rich mussels.

> *4¹/₂ pounds mussels, scrubbed and debearded just before cooking*
> *1 cup rice wine (sake or mirin)*
> *10 cloves garlic, peeled and smashed with the flat blade of a knife*
> *10 quarter-size rounds sliced gingerroot, smashed with the flat blade of a knife*
> *4 tablespoons chopped cilantro (optional)*

In a large stockpot, Dutch oven, or saucepan, combine the mussels, rice wine, garlic, and gingerroot. Bring to a boil over medium-high heat, cover, and cook 5 to 7 minutes, or until the mussels open. Shake pan occasionally during cooking to redistribute mussels.

With a slotted spoon, remove mussels that have opened and continue cooking the remaining mussels 1 to 2 minutes longer. Remove the open mussels and discard the rest.

Divide the mussels and mussel liquid among individual bowls, or transfer to one large serving bowl. If desired, sprinkle with cilantro.

Serves 4 as an entrée, 8 as an appetizer

Mussel, Potato, and Tomato Salad

YOU'LL ENJOY the combination of textures and flavors in this salad, which is best made when new potatoes are in season.

    4 1/2 pounds mussels, scrubbed and debearded just before cooking

    1/2 cup water

    2 bay leaves

    2 pounds small (1- to 1 1/2-inch) new potatoes, scrubbed

    4 green onions, top 2 inches removed, remaining portion cut into 1/4-inch slices

    2 tablespoons snipped fresh dill

    2 teaspoons Dijon mustard

    2 tablespoons white dry vermouth or defatted chicken stock

    2 tablespoons white wine vinegar

    2 tablespoons extra virgin olive oil

    Salt and freshly ground black pepper

    1 pint cherry tomatoes, rinsed

    1 pound spinach leaves, rinsed, drained, and spun dry

(continued)

MUSSEL WINES

Nicknamed "poor man's oysters," mussels taste like a cross between an oyster and a clam. Their flavor is sweet, sometimes a tad smoky, yet refined. Wines that pair well with the musky, dense meat of mussels include Chenin Blanc, Sémillon, Sauvignon Blanc–Sémillon blends, sparkling wines, and Pinot Gris. Lean, acidic Chardonnays with lemon-citrus undertones may also work, although strong, oaky, buttery Chardonnays are best avoided. Fruity red wines, such as Merlot and Zinfandel, match mussels, particularly when the shellfish is cooked in a tomato-based sauce or broth.

In a large stockpot, Dutch oven, or saucepan, combine the mussels, water, and bay leaves. Bring to a boil over medium-high heat, cover, and cook for 5 to 7 minutes, or until the mussels open. Shake the pan occasionally during cooking to redistribute the mussels.

Using a slotted spoon, remove the mussels that have opened and continue cooking the remaining mussels for 1 to 2 minutes longer. Remove the open mussels and discard any that have not opened.

Strain the mussel liquid through several layers of dampened cheesecloth and reserve 2 tablespoons of the liquid. When the mussels are cool enough to handle, remove the meat from the shells and reserve. Discard the shells.

Place the potatoes in a large saucepan and cover with cold water. Bring to a boil, cover, decrease heat to a simmer, and cook 15 to 20 minutes, or until the potatoes are tender but not mushy.

While the potatoes are cooking, make the salad dressing by whisking together the green onions, dill, mustard, vermouth, white wine vinegar, reserved 2 tablespoons mussel liquid, and olive oil in a small bowl. Season to taste with salt and pepper and reserve.

When the potatoes are done, drain them, cool slightly, and cut in half. Place the potatoes in a large nonreactive bowl. While they are still warm, pour on half the reserved dressing and toss gently to coat.

In another nonreactive bowl place the cherry tomatoes, mussels, and remaining dressing and toss gently to coat.

To serve, divide the spinach leaves among individual plates and spoon one-quarter of the mussel–tomato mixture in the center of each plate. Spoon one-quarter of the potatoes around the mussel–tomato mixture.

Serves 4

Mussels Provençal

Etta's Seafood, Seattle, Washington

THIS STEAMED MUSSEL DISH is unique because of the addition of shiitake mushrooms and kalamata olives to a tomato-wine broth.

> $1/4$ cup olive oil
>
> 1 cup shiitake mushrooms, stems removed and discarded, caps thinly sliced
>
> 4 cloves garlic, chopped
>
> 1 cup peeled, seeded, and chopped tomatoes
>
> 24 oil-cured olives, such as kalamata or niçoise, pitted
>
> 4 teaspoons chopped mixed fresh herbs, such as rosemary, sage, thyme, and/or parsley
>
> $2 1/2$ pounds mussels, scrubbed and debearded just before cooking
>
> $1/4$ lemon, cut into 2 wedges
>
> 1 cup dry white wine
>
> 2 tablespoons butter, at room temperature
>
> Sprigs of fresh rosemary and fresh thyme
>
> Salt and freshly ground black pepper

(continued)

Heat the olive oil in a large skillet or Dutch oven over medium-high heat until small bubbles form. Add the shiitake mushrooms and cook 1 to 2 minutes, stirring often. Add the garlic, tomatoes, olives, herbs, and mussels. Squeeze the lemon wedges over the contents of the pan and toss the wedges in the pan. Add the white wine, butter, and rosemary and thyme sprigs. Shake the pan or stir to mix well.

Cover and cook 5 to 7 minutes, or until the mussels open. Shake the pan occasionally during cooking to redistribute the mussels. With a slotted spoon, remove mussels that have opened and continue cooking the remaining mussels 1 to 2 minutes longer. Remove open mussels and discard the rest. Taste the broth and season with salt and pepper, if desired. (I find the olives provide enough salt and the garlic and lemon enough flavor that pepper isn't necessary.)

To serve, divide the mussels, mushrooms, olives, and broth among individual bowls, or transfer to a large serving bowl. Be sure to provide seafood forks, a shell dish, and extra napkins for handy cleanup.

Serves 2 as a light entrée, 4 as an appetizer

Mussels in Pinot Noir Butter

John Doerper, chef/author

ALTHOUGH MANY PEOPLE believe that red wines and seafood don't mix, this recipe proves them wrong with delicious results.

> *3/4 cup Oregon Pinot Noir*
> *2 dozen large mussels (about 1 1/2 pounds), scrubbed and debearded just before cooking*
> *2 tablespoons finely minced shallots*
> *2 tablespoons freshly squeezed lemon juice*
> *1/2 cup unsalted butter, cut into pieces*
> *6 tiny cornichons, cut lengthwise into quarters*

Bring 1/2 cup of the Pinot Noir to a boil in a large nonreactive saucepan or Dutch oven. Reduce the heat to medium-high, add the mussels, cover, and steam until the mussels open, about 5 to 7 minutes, shaking the pan occasionally to redistribute the mussels. With a slotted spoon, remove the mussels that have opened and continue cooking the remaining mussels 1 to 2 minutes longer. Remove open mussels and discard the rest. Reserve the mussels and cooking liquid in separate containers for later use.

While the mussels cool, place the remaining 1/4 cup Pinot Noir, the shallots, and lemon juice in a nonreactive medium skillet and reduce over low heat, about 5 to 7 minutes, or until the liquid is almost gone. Stir in the reserved mussel cooking liquid and reduce over medium heat until the liquid thickens slightly and is reduced to about 3 tablespoons. In the final stages, the liquid thickens rapidly, so watch it carefully and do not allow it to burn.

Remove the pan from the heat and add 1 or 2 small pieces of butter. Add the remaining butter one piece at a time. Whisk steadily until blended. The butter sauce should have the consistency of homemade mayonnaise, neither too solid nor too liquid. (The warm skillet should retain sufficient heat to do this smoothly; if the temperature drops too much, return the skillet to low heat. If the butter separates or curdles, whisk rapidly to emulsify.)

Remove the mussels from their shells and discard the upper shells. Place a cornichon quarter in the lower shells, place a mussel on each cornichon, and cover with sauce.

To serve, divide the mussels on individual plates or place on a large serving platter and serve immediately.

Serves 4 as an appetizer

Five-Spice Rice with Mussels

THE UNUSUAL BLENDING of Asian flavors in a traditional rice pilaf works so well with plump, buttery mussels, it is irresistible.

> *1 tablespoon peanut oil*
> *$1/4$ teaspoon toasted sesame oil*
> *3 cloves garlic, minced*
> *1 tablespoon minced gingerroot, or 1 teaspoon ground ginger*
> *1 teaspoon five-spice powder*
> *1 cup long-grain white rice*
> *2 cups fish stock, clam juice, defatted chicken stock, or water*
> *$1/8$ teaspoon salt*
> *Zest of $1/2$ orange*
> *$1/4$ cup water*
> *$2^1/2$ pounds mussels, scrubbed and debearded just before cooking*
> *Chopped cilantro, for garnish*

(continued)

In a medium saucepan, heat the peanut oil and toasted sesame oil over medium-high heat. Add the garlic and gingerroot and cook for 30 seconds, stirring continuously. Add the five-spice powder and rice and cook, stirring continuously, until the rice is evenly coated with oil and the five-spice powder is evenly distributed.

Add the fish stock, salt, and orange zest and bring to a boil. Decrease the heat to a simmer, cover, and cook until the liquid is absorbed, about 15 to 20 minutes.

About 10 minutes before the rice is done, bring the 1/4 cup water to a boil in a large saucepan. Decrease the heat to medium-high, add the mussels, cover, and cook 5 to 7 minutes, or until the mussels open. Shake the pan occasionally to redistribute the mussels. With a slotted spoon, remove the mussels that have opened and continue cooking the remaining mussels 1 to 2 minutes longer. Remove the open mussels and discard the rest.

To serve, place a mound of rice in the center of individual plates and arrange the mussels in a circular pattern around the rice. Garnish with chopped cilantro.

Serves 4

Baked Oysters

COOKED IN THEIR SHELLS on the grill, in the barbecue, or in the oven, fresh oysters are great plain or served with a bit of melted butter mixed with Tabasco, Old Bay seasoning, or *shichimi togarashi,* a flavorful Japanese spice blend.

> *Fresh oysters, shells rinsed and scrubbed*
> *Rock salt (optional)*

Preheat oven to 400°F. Place a cooling rack on a rimmed baking sheet. Alternately, sprinkle a jelly roll pan or a long, shallow pan with 1/2 inch of rock salt, which will help steady the oysters. Place the oysters rounded side down (flat side up) evenly spaced over the long, thin crossbars of the rack or the bed of rock salt.

Place the baking sheet on the center rack of the oven. Cook 7 to 15 minutes, depending on the size of the oysters, until the shells open slightly, or until steam or bubbles escape around the fluted edges. Do not turn oysters during cooking.

Using an oyster knife and an oyster mitt to protect your hands, shuck the oysters. The oysters will open easily when fully cooked. If an oyster is not done to your liking, just return it to the oven and cook an extra minute or two.

FUN FACT

On the West Coast, Native Americans came from as far north as Alaska to raid the oyster beds in Puget Sound, feasting for days after cooking the oysters over hot coals. On both the Pacific and Atlantic coasts, pre-Columbian Native Americans seem never to have eaten oysters raw, which is one of the reasons they are often credited with inventing American oyster stew.

Fried Oyster Caesar Salad

FRIED OYSTERS are inherently rich, but I assuage the guilt by serving the crispy bites with lots of greens and a lightened Caesar-style dressing for an unusual main-dish salad.

> 24 fresh oysters in the shell, or 1 (10-ounce) jar fresh shucked oysters, juice drained
> through a fine sieve and reserved
> 1 cup all-purpose flour or cornmeal
> 1 teaspoon sweet paprika
> $1/4$ teaspoon salt
> $1/4$ teaspoon freshly ground white pepper or black pepper
> Peanut oil, for frying
> 1 head romaine lettuce, rinsed, drained, spun dry, and separated into individual leaves
> 1 head red leaf lettuce, rinsed, drained, spun dry, and separated into individual leaves
> Lightened Caesar Dressing (recipe follows)

Using an oyster knife and an oyster mitt to protect your hands, shuck the oysters over a bowl to catch as much of the oyster liquor as possible. Discard the top and bottom shells, and reserve the oysters. Set aside the oyster liquor to use in the dressing.

On a piece of waxed paper, mix together the flour, sweet paprika, salt, and white pepper. Dredge the oysters in seasoned flour, then shake well to remove the excess.

Pour $1/8$ inch oil into a large skillet or wok. Heat over medium-high heat until almost smoking. Add the oysters and cook I to 2 minutes per side, or until the oysters are golden in color. Do not overcook or the oysters will become tough. As the oysters finish cooking, transfer them to a plate lined with several layers of paper towels to drain the excess oil.

Place several whole romaine and red leaf lettuce leaves on individual plates. Position 6 oysters around the perimeter of each plate, and a ramekin of Caesar dressing on the side for dunking oysters and lettuce leaves.

Serves 4

Lightened Caesar Dressing

$^1/_4$ cup defatted chicken stock
$^1/_4$ cup reserved oyster liquor (add additional chicken stock or clam juice
     to make $^1/_4$ cup, if necessary)
$^1/_4$ cup freshly squeezed lemon juice
2 tablespoons capers, minced
2 cloves garlic, minced
$^1/_4$ teaspoon salt
$^1/_2$ teaspoon freshly ground black pepper
$^1/_2$ teaspoon white or dark Worcestershire sauce
$^1/_4$ cup freshly grated Parmesan or Parmigiano-Reggiano cheese
2 tablespoons extra virgin olive oil

In a small mixing bowl or a small jar with a lid combine the chicken stock, oyster liquor, lemon juice, capers, garlic, salt, pepper, Worcestershire sauce, and Parmesan cheese. Stir or shake well. Whisk in the olive oil or shake until well blended.

Makes 1 cup

Oysters Chez Shea

Chez Shea, Pike Place Public Market

THIS RECIPE is best made in the winter months when oysters are in top form and plentiful. Serve with Champagne or sparkling wine.

> *Rock salt or dried beans*
> *12 fresh yearling oysters in the shell, shells scrubbed*
> *1/2 teaspoon vegetable oil*
> *1 1/2 teaspoons minced gingerroot*
> *1 tablespoon freshly squeezed lime juice*
> *1 cup coconut milk*
> *1 tablespoon maple syrup*
> *1/4 teaspoon crushed red pepper flakes plus additional, for garnish*
> *Salt and freshly ground black pepper*
> *2 tablespoons minced cilantro plus additional sprigs, for garnish*
> *Lime wedges*

Cover a rimmed baking sheet with 1/2 inch of rock salt or dried beans. Using an oyster knife and an oyster mitt to protect your hands, shuck the oysters over a bowl to catch as much of the oyster liquor as possible. Place the oysters in a separate bowl and refrigerate the oysters and liquor until ready to use. Reserve the bottom oyster shells. Heat a small pot of water to boiling, then boil the reserved oyster shells 2 minutes to disinfect. Drain well, dry the shells, place on the prepared baking sheet, and set aside for later use.

Heat the vegetable oil in a small saucepan over medium-high heat. Add the gingerroot and cook for 1 minute, stirring often. Add the lime juice and swirl the pan to mix. Add the coconut milk, maple syrup, 1/4 teaspoon red pepper flakes, and reserved oyster liquor. Bring the sauce to a boil, decrease the heat to a simmer, and cook 3 to 5 minutes, or until the sauce coats the back of a spoon. Season to taste with salt and black pepper.

Add the oysters to the sauce and cook 2 to 3 minutes, or until the oysters plump and edges curl. Remove from the heat and spoon the oysters into the reserved shells. Spoon additional sauce over the oysters and sprinkle with cilantro and red pepper flakes, for garnish.

To serve, divide the oysters and lime wedges among individual plates.

Serves 4 as an appetizer

OYSTER WINES

Pairing the proper wines with raw oysters on the half shell has become a passion among Northwest wine connoisseurs because it is such a delicious challenge.

Young, lean white wines with crisp acids that slice through the briny, metallic sea flavors of the oysters and refresh the palate routinely win wine-and-oyster-pairing contests. Wines that "let the oyster be an oyster" are favorites. These include Sémillon, Sémillon-Chardonnay, lighter-style Chardonnay, Sauvignon Blanc (sometimes referred to as Fumé Blanc), Sauvignon Blanc–Sémillon blends, Chenin Blanc, Pinot Gris, Melon, Riesling, and Dry Riesling. Big, buttery, oaky Chardonnays don't do as well.

Some connoisseurs prefer beer with their oysters, particularly a high-quality dark stout. Other oyster beers include porter, stout, and wheat ales.

Some people enjoy light red wines with oysters, citing Oregon Pinot Noirs as good matches. This may make more sense on reflection than it does at first blush, when you consider that mignonette (a sauce made of red wine vinegar and shallots) is a classic with oysters. Cooked oysters are easier to match with drink than raw oysters, because the seasonings that influence a recipe's flavor help determine the beverage choice.

PART IV

THE ODD KETTLE OF SEAFOOD

FROM A TO S (ALBACORE TUNA TO SQUID)

Braised Albacore Tuna with Secret Sauce

Pike Place Fish, Pike Place Public Market

PIKE PLACE FISH sells a bottled spice blend called Northwest Seafood Seasoning. It's the secret ingredient in this ruddy red sauce that goes particularly well with fresh albacore tuna.

> *1 tablespoon Northwest Seafood Seasoning (see note)*
> *1 cup dry white wine*
> *2 tablespoons unsalted butter*
> *1 1/2 pounds albacore tuna loins or steaks, rinsed, drained, patted dry,*
>   *and cut into 4 (6-ounce) pieces*

In a small bowl, stir together the Northwest Seafood Seasoning and 2 tablespoons of the white wine and reserve.

Heat butter in a large skillet over medium-high heat. When butter foams, add the tuna fillets and cook 1 to 2 minutes, or until the outside surface turns white. Turn fillets and cook another 1 to 2 minutes, or until the second side turns white. Remove tuna fillets to a plate and reserve.

Add the reserved wine mixture to the pan and stir, scraping up any browned bits of fish that have accumulated on the bottom of the pan. Add the remaining white wine and stir well. Add the tuna fillets and spoon the sauce over the fillets. Decrease the heat to medium-low, cover the pan, and cook until the tuna is pale pink in the middle, about 3 to 6 minutes depending on the thickness of the fish.

Remove the tuna fillets from the pan and reserve. Increase the heat to medium-high and reduce the sauce until thickened slightly, stirring often.

To serve, divide the tuna and sauce among individual plates.

Serves 4

Note: *Northwest Seafood Seasoning can be used in numerous ways. Add it to melted butter and lemon juice and spread on fish fillets before grilling or broiling. Sprinkle a bit in seafood soups or stews, or sprinkle some directly on fish before sautéing, baking, or poaching. Add it to flour and dredge fish before pan-frying or deep-frying. It is available at Pike Place Fish's stall under the famous Market clock or by calling (800) 542-7732.*

FUN FACT

The very dark lateral strip of meat that is found in tuna and some other types of fish (such as mackerel and swordfish) is known as red muscle and is crucial to the fish for long-range swimming. Nutritionally, it offers a high level of iron and copper, as well as higher levels of protein than the flesh that surrounds it. Its intense flavor is often described as bitter, and some people like it more than others (the Japanese often eat it for its health benefits). This part of the flesh also spoils more quickly than the surrounding meat, but if the fish is fresh and you enjoy the taste and don't mind the color, there is no reason to remove it before cooking.

Grilled Albacore Tuna Spinach Salad

TRY THIS RECIPE on meat-eaters who think they don't like fish—it's so rich they will almost believe they're eating steak!

> 2 tablespoons minced garlic
> 6 tablespoons Worcestershire sauce
> $1/2$ teaspoon Tabasco sauce
> 6 tablespoons extra virgin olive oil
> 1 $1/2$ pounds albacore tuna loins or steaks, rinsed, drained, patted dry, and cut into
>   4 (6-ounce) pieces
> 2 cups fresh mushrooms, cut in half (or quarters if extra-large)
> 1 bunch spinach leaves, rinsed, drained, tough stems removed, and well dried
> 2 carrots, cut into $1/8$-inch-wide slices
> $1/2$ red onion, cut crosswise into $1/8$-inch-wide slices

Place the garlic, Worcestershire sauce, Tabasco, and olive oil in a nonreactive mixing bowl large enough to hold the fish without crowding, and stir or whisk to blend. Divide the marinade in half. To half of the marinade, add the fish fillets, turning well to coat. To the marinade remaining in the other bowl, add the mushrooms, and stir well to coat. Cover both bowls and refrigerate 20 minutes to 2 hours, turning occasionally.

Ten minutes before cooking, heat the grill, then lightly coat the rack with oil or nonstick cooking spray. Remove fish fillets from the marinade, pat dry, and place on the grill.

Cook 3 to 5 minutes, then turn and cook another 3 to 5 minutes, about 10 minutes per inch of thickness, or just until the fish turns opaque. Discard the fish marinade.

To serve, divide the spinach leaves among individual plates. Place a fish fillet in the center of the leaves, then divide the carrot and onion slices among the plates, sprinkling the slices over the fish fillets and spinach leaves. Spoon the marinated mushrooms and any remaining marinade over and around the fish and vegetables.

Serves 4

Sablefish with Kasu Marinade

KASU IS A FRAGRANT, doughy sediment left over after rice is fermented to make sake, much like the lees, or dregs, that remain after winemaking.

> *5 teaspoons salt*
> *1 quart water*
> *1 1/4 pounds sablefish fillets, rinsed, drained, patted dry, and cut*
> *into 4 (5-ounce) pieces*
> *1 pound kasu*
> *2 tablespoons shiro (white) miso*
> *1/4 cup mirin, sake, or water*
> *1 cup shredded spinach leaves or 1/4 pound ocean salad (optional; see note)*

In a large nonreactive baking pan that will hold the sablefish fillets in 1 layer, combine the salt and water and stir until the salt is dissolved. Add the sablefish, turn to coat both sides, cover, and refrigerate. After 30 minutes, remove the pan from the refrigerator, drain the fillets, and pat dry. Rinse out the pan and dry.

(continued)

In a mixing bowl, stir together the kasu, miso, and mirin. Add the sablefish fillets to the baking pan and spread the kasu mixture evenly over the fish. Cover the sablefish with the mixture, turning to coat all sides; cover the pan and refrigerate 1 to 2 days, depending on the strength of flavor desired (marinating for 1 day gives a more subtle flavor that may work best for first-timers).

When ready to cook, preheat broiler. Lightly oil a baking sheet or spray with non-stick cooking spray.

Scrape the kasu mixture off the fillets, leaving a light film on the surface. Arrange the fish fillets on the baking sheet and place the fish 3 to 4 inches under the broiler. Broil 10 to 12 minutes per inch of thickness, or until the fish just turns opaque.

Divide the spinach among individual plates and top with fish fillets.

Serves 4

Note: Kasu *is available at Japanese markets, which also sometimes offer premarinated sablefish. All you have to do is open the package; sauté, grill, or broil; and enjoy. Ocean salad is a mixture of seaweed, kelp, and other ocean-floor greens. It is usually available fresh or frozen in seafood stores and Asian markets or specialty grocery stores. While it adds a salty taste and chewy texture, it is not essential.*

Pan-Fried Smelt with Lemon Butter

PAN-FRYING the freshest smelt is an ideal way to cook these small-in-size but big-in-flavor fish.

> *¹/₄ cup all-purpose flour*
> *¹/₄ cup cornmeal*
> *¹/₄ teaspoon salt*
> *¹/₈ teaspoon freshly ground black pepper*
> *2 pounds smelt, rinsed and patted dry*
> *4 tablespoons canola oil*
> *1 lemon, cut into 8 wedges*
> *2 tablespoons butter*

Preheat oven to 200°F.

In a large plastic bag, mix the flour, cornmeal, salt, and pepper. Add half the smelt, close the bag securely, and shake well to coat the fish with the flour mixture.

Heat 2 tablespoons of the oil in a large skillet over medium-high heat. Add the coated smelt, without crowding, and fry 3 to 4 minutes, turning once, until the cooked fish are golden brown and opaque throughout (cut into one to check for doneness). Place the smelt on a baking sheet and keep warm in the oven.

Repeat the procedure with the remaining flour mixture, smelt, and 2 tablespoons canola oil. When all the smelt are cooked, decrease the heat to medium, squeeze 4 of the lemon wedges into the oil remaining in the pan, and scrape up any cooked bits of fish or batter left in the skillet. Add butter and cook until melted, stirring well.

Divide the smelt among individual plates and drizzle the lemon butter over the fish. Serve immediately, garnishing the fish with the remaining lemon wedges.

Serves 4

FUN FACT

Smelt are members of the Osmeridae ("odorous" in Greek) family, of which there are only twelve known living species, including smelt, capelin, and eulachon. Native Americans living along large rivers have trapped, raked, or netted the highly prized eulachon for centuries. Eulachon, and particularly its vitamin D-rich oil, was a staple food for many Northwest coastal tribes. These fish were vital to the aboriginal economy not only because they represented food and fat, but also because eulachon oil and meat were carried to the interior along "grease trails"—well-beaten, well-known paths—where they were bartered with inland tribes. They also dried eulachons, inserted a wick, and used them as a light source; hence, one of their nicknames—candlefish.

Poached Sturgeon with Sorrel
and Wild Mushroom Sauce

Le Gourmand, Seattle, Washington

BRUCE NAFTALY, chef/owner of Le Gourmand, describes his sorrel and wild mushroom sauce as an easily accessible version of a complicated French sauce.

> *1 1/2 pounds sturgeon fillets, skin and bones removed, rinsed, drained, patted dry,*
> *   and cut into 4 (6-ounce) pieces*
> *1 leek, root and top 1 inch removed, cleaned, and coarsely chopped*
> *1 cup dry white wine*
> *3 sprigs thyme*
> *3 sprigs parsley*
> *Cold water*
> *Sorrel and Wild Mushroom Sauce (recipe follows)*

To poach sturgeon, place fillets in a skillet large enough to hold fish without crowding. Add the leek, wine, thyme, parsley, and enough water to cover the fillets. Bring to a boil, then decrease heat to low and cook 10 minutes, or until the fish just flakes. Place the fish on several layers of paper towels to drain or use a clean kitchen towel to blot.

To serve, place the fish fillets on warmed individual plates and spoon the Sorrel and Wild Mushroom Sauce over the fillets.

Serves 4

Sorrel and Wild Mushroom Sauce

¹/₂ cup Reduced White Wine Fish Stock (recipe follows)
2 cups heavy whipping cream, or 1 cup heavy whipping cream and 1 cup crème fraîche
¹/₄ cup dry Madeira
3/4 pound chanterelle, morel, shiitake, or oyster mushrooms, chopped
1 cup fresh sorrel chiffonade (see page 125)
Salt and freshly ground white pepper

Place a nonreactive saucepan over medium-high heat and add the stock, whipping cream, Madeira, and mushrooms. Cook 10 to 15 minutes, or until the mixture is reduced by half, stirring occasionally. Add the sorrel and cook 5 to 7 minutes, or until reduced to a sauce consistency. Season to taste with salt and pepper. Keep warm over very low heat or in a double boiler while preparing the fish.

Makes 1¹/₂ to 2 cups

Reduced White Wine Fish Stock

2 cups dry white wine
1 large leek, root and top 1 inch removed, cleaned, and coarsely chopped
1 small onion, coarsely chopped
1 pound fresh or frozen halibut bones, coarsely chopped into fist-size pieces and rinsed
Cold water

In a large stockpot or Dutch oven, combine 1 cup of the wine, the leek, and the onion over medium-high heat and bring to a boil. Reduce heat to a simmer and cook 10 minutes, or until the vegetables are tender. Add the remaining 1 cup of wine and the fish bones, and cook until the fish on the bones is partially cooked. Cover with water and bring to a boil. Skim and discard any foam or substance that rises to the surface of the stock. Reduce heat and simmer 30 minutes, continuing to skim surface of stock as needed.

Strain the stock through a wide-meshed sieve to remove the solids, then strain the stock through a fine-meshed sieve. Return the stock to the pot, increase heat to medium-high, and cook 15 to 20 minutes, or until the liquid is reduced by half. Cool, strain, and use immediately, or refrigerate or freeze until needed.

Makes 1 cup

Wild-Rice-Stuffed Trout

A HEARTY STUFFING studded with walnuts, dried cherries, and green onions goes great with the mild flavor of farm-raised trout.

> *2 tablespoons olive oil*
> *1 tablespoon unsalted butter*
> *1 onion, diced*
> *2 cloves garlic, minced*
> *1/2 red bell pepper, diced*
> *1/2 cup wild rice, rinsed and well drained*
> *3/4 cup water*
> *3/4 cup chicken stock*
> *1/4 teaspoon dried thyme, crumbled*
> *1/4 teaspoon salt*
> *1/8 teaspoon freshly ground black pepper*
> *Pinch of ground allspice*
> *1/4 cup toasted walnuts (see page 129), finely chopped*
> *1/4 cup dried cherries or dried cranberries, diced*
> *2 green onions, finely chopped*
> *4 whole, dressed trout, 3/4 pound each, rinsed, drained, and patted dry*
> *Additional salt and freshly ground black pepper*

Melt 1 tablespoon of the olive oil and the butter in a medium saucepan over medium-high heat; add the onion, garlic, and red bell pepper. Cook 10 minutes, or until the vegetables are tender, stirring occasionally. Do not allow the vegetables to brown. Add the wild rice and cook 2 minutes, stirring often to coat individual rice grains with oil.

Add the water, chicken stock, thyme, 1/4 teaspoon salt, 1/8 teaspoon pepper, and allspice and bring to a boil. Reduce heat to medium-low and simmer 45 minutes, or until rice kernels blossom and the rice is tender. Remove the rice from the heat, drain off any excess water, and stir in the walnuts, dried cherries, and green onions.

Ten minutes before cooking the fish, preheat oven to 350°F. Lightly coat a baking sheet large enough to hold the trout without crowding with oil or nonstick cooking spray.

Sprinkle inside the cavities of the fish lightly with salt and pepper. Spoon one-quarter of the stuffing into the cavity of each fish and place on the prepared baking sheet. Brush the outside of the trout with the remaining 1 tablespoon olive oil and cook 18 to 20 minutes, or until the trout are opaque through the thickest part (just behind the head).

Divide the trout among individual plates and serve immediately.

Serves 4

Steelhead Fillets in Basil Rice Paper

RICE PAPER, a Vietnamese staple, becomes pliable when moistened. Wrap softened sheets around steelhead fillets, then cook in a hot skillet. As if by magic, the rice paper fuses to the surface of the fish, creating a crisp texture and sweet taste.

> *16 to 24 fresh basil leaves, rinsed, drained, and patted dry*
> *4 (6-ounce) steelhead fillets, skin and bones removed, rinsed, drained, and patted dry*
> *4 pieces rice paper*
> *1 tablespoon sesame oil*
> *Vietnamese Dipping Sauce (see page 42)*

Place 2 or 3 basil leaves (depending on size) on the top and bottom of each of the fish fillets, pressing in the leaves to adhere to the surface of the fish. The leaves should not cover the fillets completely; there should still be fish flesh showing between and around the outer edges of the leaves.

Pour 1/4 inch warm water onto a plate. Place 1 piece of rice paper in the water and allow to soak for 30 seconds to 1 minute, or until pliable. Do not allow to soak too long or the rice paper will tear. Transfer the rice paper to a dry plate. Repeat with the remaining rice paper.

Place a fish fillet in the center of the rice paper, fold the ends of the rice paper to the center of the fillet until they overlap, then repeat with the opposing ends. Turn the fillet over and place on another dry plate. Repeat procedure with the remaining fillets.

Over medium heat, place a nonstick skillet large enough to hold the fillets without crowding. When the pan is hot, add the oil. When the oil is hot, add the fillets, decrease heat to medium-low, and cook 3 to 5 minutes, depending on the thickness of the fish. Turn the fish, being careful not to tear the rice paper, and finish cooking

WINES FOR THE ODD KETTLE OF SEAFOOD

Although there are no hard-and-fast rules with these unusual seafoods, some wines and beers may pair better with them than others. Sablefish is distinguished for its high oil content, soft white flesh, and large flaky texture. The recipe on page 91, Sablefish with Kasu Marinade, emphasizes the buttery texture of the fish with an Asian marinade. It pairs particularly well with a high-quality sake (served chilled) or slightly sweet sparkling wine.

Smelt are also very high in oil content, and their meat is white and rich but still delicate in flavor. When fried, as in the recipe on page 93, smelt cry out for a dry white wine, such as Chenin Blanc, Sémillon, or Sauvignon Blanc, although a dry sparkling wine or Champagne also pairs nicely with fried foods.

The meat of the white sturgeon is revered for its distinctive flavor and firm texture, which some people compare to veal. Its dense, slightly herbaceous flavor is enhanced by the earthy notes of an Oregon Pinot Noir.

Trout can be cooked in so many ways (fried, blackened, sauced) that it is probably best to match a wine to the preparation or seasonings as opposed to the tender, sweet flesh.

Tuna is known as the "sirloin of the sea" for its steak-like meatiness. Albacore, or "white meat" tuna, has become a summertime favorite on Northwest grills thanks to its ready availability, dense texture, and distinct flavor. Grilled albacore holds up well to more robust red wines, especially Merlot, Zinfandel, and Syrah. Grilled albacore is the perfect reason for drinking red wine with fish.

another 3 to 5 minutes. You will see the steelhead change from translucent to opaque as it cooks. If unsure about doneness, check by carefully cutting into the middle of one of the packets with the tip of a small, sharp knife.

To serve, divide the steelhead packets among warmed individual plates and drizzle with the Vietnamese Dipping Sauce.

Serves 4

Scallops St. Jacques

Pure Food Fish, Pike Place Public Market

THIS RECIPE combines the best aspects of the elegant French *coquilles St. Jacques* and the homey English shepherd's pie.

> 3 slices meaty bacon (optional)
> 1 cup heavy whipping cream
> 2 tablespoons unsalted butter
> 3 cloves garlic, minced
> 1/3 cup dry white wine
> 1/4 teaspoon salt
> 1/8 teaspoon freshly ground white pepper
> 1 pound Alaskan weathervane scallops, rinsed, drained, patted dry, and cut into
>   bite–size pieces
> 1 cup shucked fresh peas or thawed frozen peas
> 2 cups cooked mashed potatoes, seasoned to taste with additional salt and pepper

Preheat oven to 350°F. Lightly grease a casserole dish that will hold the scallops in a single layer with butter or spray with nonstick cooking spray. Set aside. If using bacon, cook in a small skillet over medium–high heat until well browned. Crumble and set aside.

Place the whipping cream, butter, garlic, and wine in a medium saucepan and bring to a boil over medium-high heat. Boil gently until the mixture is reduced by half, stirring frequently so the cream does not boil over, then remove the pan from the heat and stir in the 1/4 teaspoon salt and 1/8 teaspoon pepper. Add the bacon (if using), scallops, and peas, stirring to coat the ingredients completely with cream sauce.

Pour the scallop mixture into the prepared casserole dish and cover completely with the mashed potatoes. Bake 15 minutes, or until the mashed potatoes begin to look dry. Switch the oven to broil and broil the potatoes 3 to 4 inches from the heat source until they turn golden brown around the edges, about 5 minutes.

Bring the casserole to the table and serve family style.

Serves 4

WINES FOR SQUID

On its own, squid is a rather bland food, so when pairing it with wine (or beer) it may be easier to pair the wine with the cooking technique and/or sauce used, rather than the squid itself. For example, fried squid, a popular rendition, may work best with sweeter wines, such as Riesling and Gewürztraminer, or beer. Sparkling wine or Champagne is my personal favorite with fried seafood, since the bubbles cut through the fatty crust and help refresh the palate between bites.

Squid is often prepared in Italian recipes, and a spicy Zinfandel or Merlot would work with squid cooked in Italian-inspired tomato-based sauces or stocks. Spicy, sweet wines such as Riesling, Gewürztraminer, or White Zinfandel make good partners with Asian-leaning treatments of squid. Even a slightly chilled Merlot or a light-bodied Chardonnay can work with Asian-inspired squid dishes.

Vietnamese-Style Squid

THIS RECIPE uses the dipping sauce *(nuoc cham)* that comes as a condiment with Vietnamese spring rolls as a marinade for cooked squid, which soaks up more of the robust flavor the longer it marinates.

1 pound whole cleaned squid, bodies cut into 1/2-inch rings, large tentacles cut in half

3 tablespoons unseasoned rice vinegar

1 tablespoon Vietnamese fish sauce (nuoc nam)

2 1/2 tablespoons water

1 1/2 teaspoons grated gingerroot

Pinch of crushed red pepper flakes

1 clove garlic, minced

1 tablespoon sugar

1 teaspoon freshly squeezed lime juice

4 large, soft lettuce leaves, such as Bibb, red or green leaf, or iceberg

2 cups fresh bean sprouts, rinsed, drained, and patted dry

2 carrots, julienned

1 red bell pepper, seeded and julienned

1/4 cup chopped unsalted peanuts, for garnish

2 tablespoons minced cilantro or fresh mint, for garnish (optional)

Bring a large pot of water to a boil. Add the squid and cook 1 to 2 minutes, or until the squid just turns opaque. Drain into a colander and rinse immediately with cold water to stop the cooking process. Drain well and set aside.

(continued)

In a medium mixing bowl, combine the rice vinegar, fish sauce, water, gingerroot, red pepper flakes, garlic, sugar, and lime juice and stir until the sugar is dissolved. Add the squid and toss to coat evenly with the marinade. Cover the bowl and refrigerate at least 1 hour and up to 2 days, turning the bowl occasionally to redistribute the marinade.

When ready to serve, place lettuce leaves on 4 individual plates, or arrange on a large platter. Layer the bean sprouts, carrots, and red bell pepper over the lettuce leaves. Divide the squid and place on top of the vegetables. Sprinkle with peanuts and cilantro, if desired.

Serves 4

Florentine Stuffed Squid

SQUID TUBES make natural receptacles for stuffings, which are easily created with leftovers such as cooked rice or pasta; or with bread crumbs, pine nuts, hazelnuts, or almonds; cottage, Parmesan, or feta cheese; and fresh or dried herbs.

8 large whole squid bodies, about 5 or 6 inches long, cleaned and tentacles reserved

1/2 cup cooked long-grain white or brown rice

1/4 cup small-curd cottage cheese

1/4 cup freshly grated Parmesan cheese

2 tablespoons minced fresh spinach

2 tablespoons toasted pine nuts (see page 129)

2 cloves garlic, minced

1 egg, beaten

1/4 teaspoon ground nutmeg

2 tablespoons olive oil

Salt and freshly ground black pepper

1 cup homemade or store-bought marinara sauce or spaghetti sauce
1/2 cup dry white or red wine or chicken stock
Basil leaves, for garnish

Preheat oven to 325°F. Use a baking dish that will hold the squid in 1 layer, and grease lightly with butter or spray with nonstick cooking spray.

Leave the squid bodies whole. Finely chop the tentacles, and combine in a medium bowl with the rice, cottage cheese, Parmesan cheese, spinach, pine nuts, garlic, egg, nutmeg, and olive oil until well blended. Season with salt and pepper.

Spoon the stuffing into the squid bodies until they are about 3/4 full. Be careful not to overstuff as the squid will shrink when cooked and may burst if overstuffed. Close each opening with a toothpick or wooden skewer broken into thirds.

In a medium bowl, combine marinara sauce and wine. Spoon 1/4 inch of the sauce over bottom of prepared baking dish. Arrange stuffed squid in a single layer over sauce, then pour remaining sauce over top. Cover baking dish and bake for 30 to 35 minutes. Remove cover and bake another 15 minutes, or until squid is tender.

Divide the stuffed squid among individual plates and garnish with basil leaves.

Serves 4

SEAFOOD COMBINATION DISHES

Seafood Chili

MY FRIEND AND FELLOW FOODIE, Nancy Sutter, recommends using any firm fleshy whitefish, such as halibut, in this recipe. I've substituted Dungeness crab, Alaskan spot prawns, and Alaskan weathervane scallops with great results.

3 slices bacon, plus reserved bacon grease or 1 1/2 tablespoons vegetable oil

2 large onions, chopped

3 cloves garlic, minced

2 cups chopped fresh tomatoes or well-drained canned tomatoes, plus additional
for garnish

1 1/2 teaspoons chili powder

1/2 teaspoon ground cumin

1 teaspoon chopped fresh oregano, or 1/2 teaspoon dried oregano, crumbled

1 (7-ounce) can whole mild green chiles, drained and chopped, or

2 (4-ounce) cans diced mild green chiles, drained

3/4 teaspoon Tabasco sauce

1 to 1 1/4 cups dry red wine or water

1/2 pound uncooked or cooked halibut, or other firm, fleshy whitefish fillets,
skin and bones removed, cut into 1 1/2-inch chunks

1 tablespoon olive oil

1 (15 1/4-ounce) can red kidney beans, drained, rinsed, and drained again

Sour cream, for garnish

Chopped parsley, for garnish

Cook the bacon over medium heat until crisp. Place the bacon slices on a paper towel to drain and pour $1^1/_2$ tablespoons bacon grease (or vegetable oil) into a large saucepan or Dutch oven. Add the onions and garlic and cook over medium-high heat 5 to 7 minutes, or until the onions are translucent, stirring occasionally.

Add the tomatoes, chili powder, cumin, oregano, mild green chiles, and Tabasco and stir well. Add 1 cup of the red wine, bring to a boil, then decrease the heat and simmer 35 minutes, uncovered, stirring occasionally. If the mixture becomes too dry, add more red wine 1 tablespoon at a time, stirring well after each addition.

After the mixture has simmered 35 minutes, crumble the bacon and add to the chili. If using uncooked fish, add to the chili and stir gently to mix. Cook just until the fish is translucent, about 5 to 7 minutes. If using cooked fish, cook the bacon an additional 5 minutes after adding it, then add the fish and cook 2 to 3 minutes, or until the fish is warmed through.

Meanwhile, heat the olive oil in a medium skillet over medium-high heat and sauté the kidney beans until warmed through, about 3 minutes.

When the fish is cooked or warmed through, place the chili on individual plates with a spoonful of sautéed beans beside it. Top with a dollop of sour cream, and sprinkle with additional chopped tomatoes and parsley.

Serves 4

No-Bake Seafood Lasagne

THIS LAVISH ENTRÉE is special enough for company yet saves many steps and lots of time over traditional lasagna recipes because the dish is never baked.

> 8 uncooked plain or whole-wheat lasagna noodles
> 1 tablespoon olive oil
> 1/2 white or yellow onion, diced
> 1/4 pound assorted wild mushrooms (such as shiitake, cremini, oyster, porcini,
>   or portobello), sliced
> 1 plum tomato, cored and diced
> 1 cup homemade or store-bought marinara sauce or spaghetti sauce
> 2 teaspoons minced fresh basil, or 1/2 teaspoon dried basil, crumbled
> 2 pounds mussels, scrubbed and debearded just before cooking
> 1/2 pound halibut fillet, skin and bones removed, rinsed, drained, patted dry,
>   and cut into bite-size pieces
> 1/4 pound Dungeness crabmeat, picked over for shells and cartilage
> Freshly ground black pepper
> 1 ounce Parmesan or Parmigiano-Reggiano cheese (optional)

Cook the lasagna noodles according to package directions. Drain the noodles and keep warm while preparing the rest of the dish.

In a large skillet, heat the olive oil over medium-high heat. Add the onion and mushrooms and cook 5 to 7 minutes, or until the onion is tender and the mushrooms release their juices. Stir in the tomato, marinara sauce, and 1 teaspoon of the fresh basil (or all of the dried basil). Stir well and cook 2 minutes.

Add the mussels to the tomato sauce and cook 3 minutes, then add the halibut and cook for 4 minutes, stirring occasionally. Add the Dungeness crab and cook for 1 to 2 minutes more, until the mussels open and the crabmeat is heated through, removing any mussels that do not open.

To serve, arrange 2 lasagna noodles on each plate so that the noodles curl over each other and are raised in spots (do not place lasagna noodles flat on the plate). Divide sauce and seafood over noodles. Sprinkle with pepper and the remaining 1 teaspoon minced fresh basil. If desired, using a sharp vegetable peeler, shave strips of cheese over pasta and seafood (though Italians consider it blasphemy to mix cheese and seafood!).

Serves 4

WINES FOR SEAFOOD COMBINATION DISHES

The possibilities of seafood combination dishes are myriad, thus it is difficult to generalize about pairing them with wines. However, in a cioppino-and-wine-pairing contest held in downtown Seattle at Elliott's Oyster House & Seafood Restaurant, two Merlots, a Fumé Blanc, and a Chardonnay took home the top prizes. Next time you whip up a batch of hearty fisherman's stew, you might try any of these varieties of wine.

Fruity red wines, such as Merlot and Zinfandel, work well with tomato-based Italian and Mediterranean-influenced dishes. Asian beer or sweet white wines, such as Gewürztraminer or Riesling, are frequently paired with spicy Asian-inspired seafood combos. Seafoods mixed with vegetables, grains, and beans may pair advantageously with medium-dry white wines, such as Pinot Gris (Pinot Grigio in Italian), Sémillon, or Sauvignon Blanc. The earthy flavor and meaty texture of cooked lentils pairs well with the earthy aspects of Pinot Noir, which many wine experts consider to be one of the most seafood-friendly red wines.

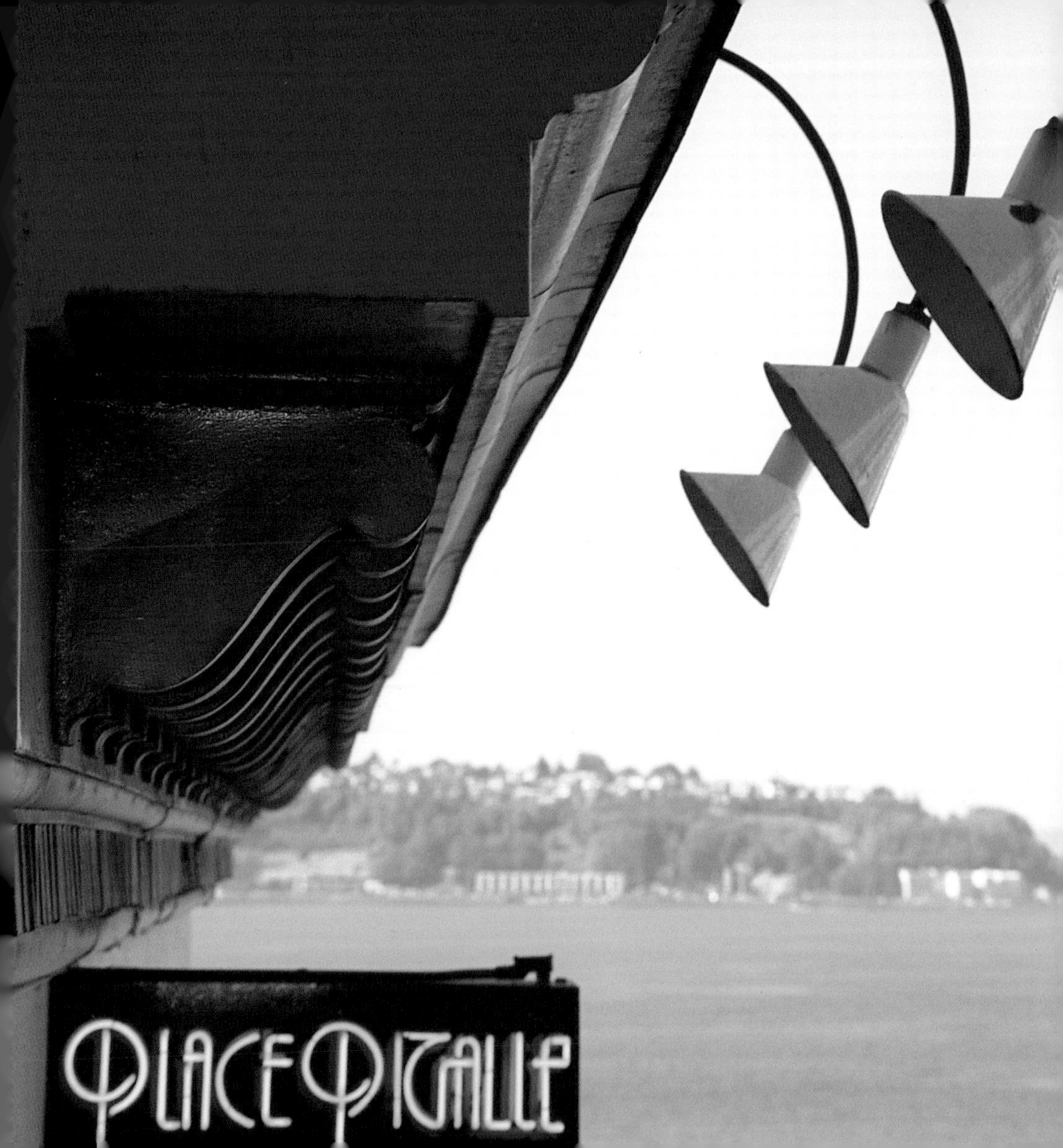
PLACE PIGALLE

Shellfish Risotto

COOKING RISOTTO has taken on a mystique that frightens away many home cooks, but it is really more forgiving than many people believe. Simply stir the risotto often and do not ever allow the stock to boil away entirely.

> 4 cups homemade chicken, fish, or vegetable stock, or 1 (14^1/$_2$-ounce) can chicken
>   stock plus 2 cups water
> ^{1}/$_2$ pound Alaskan spot prawns, peeled, deveined, rinsed, patted dry, and cut in half
>   lengthwise, shells reserved
> 1 tablespoon olive oil
> ^{1}/$_2$ white or yellow onion, minced
> 1 clove garlic, minced
> 1 ^{1}/$_2$ cups uncooked Arborio rice
> ^{1}/$_2$ cup dry white wine or white dry vermouth
> ^{1}/$_2$ pound halibut fillet, skin and bones removed, rinsed, drained, patted dry, and
>   cut into bite-size pieces
> ^{1}/$_4$ pound cleaned squid, bodies sliced into ^{1}/$_4$-inch rings, tentacles cut in half if large
> 1 tablespoon unsalted butter
> Salt and freshly ground white pepper
> 2 tablespoons minced fresh basil, for garnish

In a medium saucepan, heat the chicken stock until it comes to a simmer. Add the reserved spot prawn shells and cook 10 minutes. With a slotted spoon, remove the shells and discard. Keep the stock warm over low heat, but do not boil or reduce.

(continued)

Heat the olive oil in a large saucepan over medium-high heat. Add the onion and garlic and cook 2 to 3 minutes, stirring occasionally. Add the rice and stir to coat the grains evenly with oil. Add the wine and cook until the wine is almost totally absorbed, stirring often, about 1 to 2 minutes.

Stir in 1 cup of the warm stock. Simmer slowly, stirring often, about 6 minutes, or until the liquid is almost totally absorbed. Adjust the heat if necessary so that the liquid does not evaporate too quickly.

Continue adding stock in $1/2$-cup increments, stirring continuously until almost absorbed. When only about 1 cup of the stock remains, add the spot prawns and halibut and repeat the simmering and stirring procedure with another $1/2$ cup of the stock.

FUN FACT

Giant squid are believed to be the largest of all the world's creatures that have no backbones, growing up to 60 or 70 feet in length, longer than a city bus. Their eyes are the largest in the animal kingdom, reaching the size of dinner plates. Some of their nerve fibers are so big they were initially mistaken for blood vessels. Giant squid are inedible, however, because of a high level of ammonia in their bodies.

The rice should now be creamy in consistency and cooked al dente (firm to the bite), and the seafood should be partially cooked. If the rice is too moist, continue cooking. If too dry, add a bit more stock and continue stirring and simmering until the proper consistency is reached. Add the squid and cook 1 to 2 minutes more. Remove from the heat, add the butter, stir well, and season to taste with salt and pepper.

Divide risotto among individual bowls and sprinkle with basil. Serve immediately.

Serves 4

SEAFOOD SIDEKICKS (SAUCES)

Champagne Sauce

THIS IS A LIGHT, golden-colored cream sauce with a mild Champagne flavor.

> 2 tablespoons butter
> 2 tablespoons minced shallots
> 1/2 cup fish stock, bottled clam juice, or chicken stock
> 1/2 cup heavy whipping cream
> 1/2 cup Champagne or sparkling wine
> 1/8 teaspoon salt
> 1/8 teaspoon freshly ground white pepper

In a small skillet, melt the butter over medium-high heat. Add the shallots and cook 2 minutes, or until translucent, stirring occasionally. Add the stock, bring to a boil, and cook 5 minutes, or until reduced to 1/4 cup, stirring occasionally. Add the whipping cream and Champagne and cook 10 to 15 minutes more, or until thickened, stirring occasionally. Add the salt and white pepper, stir well, and serve over cooked fish fillets, fish steaks, or shellfish.

Makes 2/3 cup

Seafood Suggestions: *Alaskan spot prawns, halibut, salmon*

Micks' Peppery Fish Glaze

Micks' Peppouri, Pike Place Public Market

PEPPER JELLIES TENDERIZE, season, and glaze in one easy step, so they are a boon to the home cook as well as the professional chef. They are available at the Micks' permanent stand in the Market, or at micks.com.

>*¹/₄ cup Micks' pepper jelly or your choice of jalapeño jelly*
>*1 tablespoon water*

In a small saucepan, heat the pepper jelly and water over low heat just until the jelly melts, stirring often. Remove from the heat.

Lightly brush the tops of the fish fillets, steaks, or shellfish with the glaze and broil or bake until the seafood reaches desired doneness, brushing lightly with glaze every 2 to 3 minutes. Transfer the seafood to warmed dinner plates and serve immediately.

Makes ¹/₄ cup

Variations: *For a more complex sauce, mix the pepper jelly of your choice with an equal amount of orange marmalade (I like to use a low-sugar variety for a less sweet taste), then season to taste with Worcestershire sauce. Pepper jellies are also good served alongside crab cakes, added to stir-fry marinades, or thinned with a bit more water and used as a dipping sauce for fried seafood.*

Seafood Suggestions: *Alaskan spot prawns, halibut, raw oysters on the half shell, salmon*

Simple Soy Glaze

THIS SUPER-SIMPLE GLAZE (only five ingredients) is superb for summer salmon on the grill, but it is so versatile you can use it on almost any fish or shellfish you choose.

1 tablespoon light cooking oil, such as canola, safflower, corn, soy, or vegetable

1 tablespoon soy sauce or low-sodium soy sauce

1 tablespoon honey, brown sugar, or maple syrup

1 tablespoon Dijon mustard

1 1/2 teaspoons prepared horseradish

In a small bowl, mix together the oil, soy sauce, honey, and mustard. Add the horseradish and blend thoroughly.

Lightly oil a broiling pan with a rack, or spray with nonstick cooking spray. Place the fish fillets, steaks, or shellfish on the rack and brush lightly with glaze. Broil 3 to 4 inches from the heat source for 3 minutes, then brush the fillets again. If the seafood starts to brown too much, move the pan 4 to 6 inches from the heat source. Continue brushing at 3-minute intervals and cook until the seafood reaches desired doneness.

Makes 1/4 cup

Variation: *If you don't like horseradish, you can substitute freshly grated gingerroot, Chinese five-spice powder, Japanese seven-spice seasoning* (shichimi togarashi), *or hot chile oil for an Asian flair. Cajun blackening mix creates a southern touch. Add the alternative seasonings a little at a time, until you reach the level of spiciness or hotness you prefer.*

Seafood Suggestions: *Alaskan spot prawns, albacore tuna steaks, halibut, salmon*

Basic Homemade Mayonnaise and Variations

HOMEMADE MAYONNAISE is a cinch to make and tastes much better than store-bought versions. Experiment by adding fresh or dried herbs, ground spices, chutneys, salsas, or capers.

> *1 large egg, at room temperature*
> *1 teaspoon Dijon mustard*
> *1/8 teaspoon kosher salt*
> *1/8 teaspoon freshly ground white pepper*
> *1 cup vegetable, canola, or mild olive oil, or a mixture of 1/2 cup mild olive oil and*
> *1/2 cup vegetable or canola oil, at room temperature*
> *1 teaspoon to 1 tablespoon freshly squeezed lemon juice, white wine vinegar, or*
> *tarragon vinegar*

Place the egg, mustard, salt, and pepper in a medium nonreactive mixing bowl and whisk until the mixture begins to lighten in color. Add the oil drop by drop, whisking constantly, stirring in the same direction and at the same speed.

When the mayonnaise begins to thicken, add the oil more quickly, in a thin stream. When the oil is incorporated and the mayonnaise is thick and smooth, season to taste with lemon juice or vinegar. If the mixture is too thick, thin with a bit of hot water to the desired consistency.

Makes 1 cup

Variations: *Add minced fresh herbs, such as tarragon, chives, basil, dill, cilantro, thyme, mint, or garlic. Or cook some curry powder or chili powder in a small amount of oil, allow to cool, then add mayonnaise and stir well to make curry or chili mayonnaise. Citrus juices, such as lime or orange, add another dimension to the mayonnaise. Fresh green, yellow, orange, or red bell peppers, finely diced, add beautiful color, taste, and* *texture to basic mayonnaise, and roasted peppers add a smoky taste and lush texture. A bit of pesto sauce also works well. Other additions to flavor mayonnaise include chutneys, salsas, gingerroot or dried ginger, green or black olives, or mustards of all types, including honey mustard or country-style (grainy) mustard.*

To make your own homemade **tartar sauce,** *add diced gherkins or sweet pickles, minced capers, a pinch of paprika, minced green olives, and diced parsley to the basic mayonnaise.*

A mock **aïoli** *sauce can be made by adding fresh garlic cloves that have been peeled and crushed with a mortar and pestle, or roasted garlic that has been squeezed out of its shell and crushed with the back of a spoon.*

A tangy **rémoulade** *sauce is made by adding diced capers, diced dill pickles, additional Dijon mustard, and chopped green onion to the basic mayonnaise.*

Green Goddess *dressing is a mixture of mayonnaise and thinly sliced green onions, watercress, or spinach leaves (or fresh parsley, top curly parts only; or fresh dill, feathery parts only), and Worcestershire sauce or anchovy fillets.*

Romesco Sauce

THIS RICH CRIMSON SAUCE hails from Catalonia, Spain. Traditionally, it is served with grilled or broiled fish; I also like it with shellfish. Be sure to use a good-quality, fruity olive oil—preferably Spanish, of course.

> *1 very ripe tomato, cored and coarsely chopped*
> *4 cloves garlic, cut in half*
> *1/3 cup toasted whole almonds (see page 129)*
> *2 slices white bread, crusts removed, crumbled*
> *1/4 teaspoon crushed red pepper flakes*
> *1/4 teaspoon (or more) ground hot paprika*
> *1/4 teaspoon (or more) salt*
> *1/4 cup (or more) red wine vinegar*
> *1/4 cup olive oil*

Place the tomato, garlic, almonds, bread, red pepper flakes, paprika, salt, and vinegar in a food processor or blender and process until only very small pieces remain.

Add the olive oil in a thin, steady stream until the mixture is smooth and thickened. Season to taste with additional salt, paprika, or red wine vinegar, if desired. Serve with simply grilled, broiled, or baked finfish or selected shellfish.

Makes 1 1/4 cups

Seafood Suggestions: *Alaskan spot prawns, Bay shrimp, clams, halibut, mussels, trout*

APPENDIX

TECHNIQUES

BEFORE BEGINNING TO COOK, read through the recipe a couple of times to familiarize yourself with the cooking techniques, steps involved, and ingredients required. Thoroughly understanding the road map of a recipe before diving in can save lots of wasted effort and poor results later on. *Mise en place* is a French cooking term (pronounced "MEEZ ahn plahs") that refers to having all the ingredients prepared and ready to combine before starting to cook. It is useful for any dish, but particularly for seafood sautés, stir-fries, or other dishes that are cooked over high heat in a short amount of time.

Where recipes do not specify options, use the following:

- Fresh herbs

- Freshly ground black or white pepper

- Medium-size fruits and vegetables, unless stated otherwise

- Granulated (white) sugar

- Kosher salt, not table salt (which contains chemicals and additives that give it a harsh, cloying taste)

- Large eggs

- Unsalted butter or margarine

- Unsifted, all-purpose (white) flour

- Whole milk

- Whole-milk yogurt

- White baking potatoes

THE RECIPES IN THIS BOOK are designed to yield four servings unless otherwise noted. Four was chosen as an average number, and the serving size is considered average, although it may provide more or less than you would like. If you are cooking for two, almost all of the recipes can be cut in half and cooked as directed. If cooking for six or eight, most recipes can be doubled or tripled, although slight adjustments in cooking times or the addition of increased amounts of seasonings will sometimes be necessary.

The recipes rarely require more than basic cooking techniques and terms. However, I do use a few techniques and terms that are less common and warrant some description. Here are the ones that might be unfamiliar.

Chiffonade: Pull basil or sorrel leaves from their stems, stack neatly one on top of another, and roll tightly like a cigar. Using a very sharp knife, cut into thin slivers. Unroll the slivers, fluff, and measure.

Clarifying butter (ghee): Melt unsalted butter in a nonstick skillet over low heat. As the white foam rises to the top, skim and discard it. The clarified butter is the heavy yellow liquid that remains in the bottom of the pan.

Deglazing: After you sauté or roast a food, a flavorful residue of browned juices and food particles sticks to the bottom and sides of the pan. To make a delicious sauce from these caramelized pan juices, add a small amount of liquid (such as wine, broth, or water) to the hot pan and heat on the stove top over medium-high heat. With a wooden spoon or spatula, scrape the bottom and sides of the pan to loosen the browned particles and crusted juices. The sauce can be served as is, or additional ingredients may be added.

Degreasing: For health and/or aesthetic reasons, it is sometimes preferable to remove excess fat from the surface of sauces, soups, stocks, or stews before serving. Several

times as the liquid cooks, simply draw a large spoon over its surface, removing a thin layer of fat and discarding it. After the dish is cooked, remove the pan from the heat and let it sit for 5 minutes. Any remaining fat will rise to the surface, where it may be removed by drawing a paper towel across the surface. Another way to degrease (if time permits) is to chill the food in the refrigerator or freezer until the grease congeals on top, then remove it with a spoon.

Making unseasoned soft bread crumbs: Tear a slice of white or whole wheat bread into chunks and place in a food processor. Process until crumbs of the desired size form. Fresh bread crumbs can be stored in the refrigerator for up to a week; in the freezer, tightly wrapped, they keep for about six months.

Making unseasoned dry bread crumbs: Place a layer of white or whole wheat bread slices on a baking sheet and bake at 300°F for 10 to 15 minutes, or until the bread turns light brown and dries completely. Allow the bread to cool, then place in a food processor or blender and process until you have the desired texture.

Making unseasoned dry bread cubes: Remove crusts from several slices of white or whole wheat bread. Cut the slices into $1/4$-inch cubes. Place a single layer of bread cubes on a baking sheet and bake at 300°F until the cubes turn light brown and dry completely, about 10 to 15 minutes. Toss during cooking. Allow the cubes to cool and use immediately; refrigerate for up to a week; or freeze, tightly wrapped, for up to 6 months.

Peeling and seeding a tomato: Cut a shallow X in the bottom end of the tomato and drop into boiling water for 15 to 20 seconds. Remove and transfer to a bowl of ice water. Remove, pat dry, and slip off skins with a sharp knife. To seed, cut each tomato in half horizontally and gently squeeze the halves over a bowl to force out the seeds. Fingers or a small spoon work well to remove any remaining seeds.

Plumping dried fruits: Add fruits to a small saucepan and cover with water, stock, or liqueur. Bring to a boil, cover, then remove the pan from the heat. Allow to stand for 20 minutes, or until the fruit is plumped. To speed the plumping process, put $^1/_2$ cup water in a microwave-safe glass dish. Add the fruit and microwave on HIGH for 30 seconds. Stir and repeat. When the fruit begins to plump, remove from the microwave and cover. Let rest for 5 minutes, drain water, then use the fruit as directed.

Reducing sauces: Reducing, or cooking down liquids of a sauce, concentrates the flavors and thickens the sauce to the right consistency. Do not further salt a liquid or sauce that is to be reduced, or the final sauce may end up oversalted. Season to taste after the sauce has been reduced.

Roasting garlic: Preheat oven to 375°F. Slice $^1/_2$ inch off the top of the garlic bulb, wrap in aluminum foil, and bake for 35 minutes.

Roasting bell peppers: Roasting peppers can be done in one of four ways. Char the skin of whole peppers with a propane blowtorch until the skin is black; roast the peppers over a gas burner on high heat, turning frequently with kitchen tongs, until well charred on all sides; broil the peppers under a broiler several inches from the heat until brownish-black blisters form; or roast the peppers in a 400°F oven for 10 to 15 minutes until dark blisters form.

Put roasted peppers in a paper or plastic bag, close the top, and let stand for 10 minutes. Remove the peppers from the bag and scrape off the skin, then cut in half and remove the seeds and ribs. Wipe away any remaining black particles with a damp cloth, then slice or chop as needed. If desired, use latex or rubber gloves to protect your hands while preparing the peppers.

Toasting hazelnuts: Place nuts on a baking sheet in a single layer and toast in a 375°F oven for 10 minutes. Remove from the oven and allow to cool slightly. Place the nuts between two rough kitchen towels and rub off as much of the brown skins as you can, or rub a handful of nuts between your palms, or a single difficult-to-skin nut between your forefinger and thumb. Alternatively (particularly for small quantities of nuts), use the toasting method described below.

Toasting sesame seeds, mustard seeds, coriander seeds, cumin seeds, and nuts: Place seeds or nuts in a dry nonstick skillet over medium heat, shaking the pan often until they begin to turn light brown or become aromatic, or both (mustard seeds will also begin to pop), about 3 to 5 minutes. Let cool, and grind as directed or add whole to your recipe.